James Caird

Landed Interest and the Supply of Food

James Caird

Landed Interest and the Supply of Food

ISBN/EAN: 9783744645638

Printed in Europe, USA, Canada, Australia, Japan

Cover: Foto ©ninafisch / pixelio.de

More available books at **www.hansebooks.com**

THE

LANDED INTEREST

AND

THE SUPPLY OF FOOD.

BY

JAMES CAIRD, C.B., F.R.S.,

Author of "English Agriculture in 1850 and 1851."

CASSELL PETTER & GALPIN:
LONDON, PARIS & NEW YORK.

PREFACE.

This Treatise was prepared at the request of the President and Council of the Royal Agricultural Society of England, to exhibit a general view of British Agriculture, for the information of European Agriculturists at the International Agricultural Congress of Paris, in 1878. For this purpose it was translated into French by M. de la Tréhonnais, and so published in Paris. It will be included, with other contributions on analogous subjects, in the forthcoming number of the *Journal of the Royal Agricultural Society*. A chapter on the future of the Landed Interests of this country has now been added, and as the subject is one of general concern, an Edition in this form has been prepared.

J. C.

8, Queen's Gate Gardens,
London, *September*, 1878.

CONTENTS.

CHAPTER I.

Home and Foreign Supply of Food.

PAGE

Functions of Government in regard to the Supply of Food—Value of Cereal and Animal Food imported from Abroad—Rapid Rise in the Value of Meat—may be checked by Importations from America—Proportion of Home and Foreign Supply of Food in this Country—England now chiefly dependent on Foreign Supplies for further Increase—Cost of Carriage equal to the Rent of Land here—Agricultural Statistics sufficiently accurate for use—Their main Features—Diminution of Corn in Ireland—Present Agricultural Prosperity of that Country—Extent of the various Crops and Numbers of Live-stock—Quantities and Value of Home and Foreign Produce, respectively, consumed annually in this Country... ... ... 1—15

CHAPTER II.

Changes and Progress in Agriculture in recent Years.

PAGE

Reaping and Mowing Machines—Steam-plough—Double-Furrow Plough—General use of Steam-power—Successive Corn-crops—use to which this might be put in time of War—capable of checking a permanent great Rise in Price of Wheat—Autumn Culture and Steam-power, with imported Manures, have given great command of Crops—Mr. Lawes' Experiments: their Value and some of their special Lessons—The Experiments at Woburn—Extension of Land-drainage and Improvement of Farm Buildings and Labourers' Cottages—Change within 30 years, more in general diffusion of Improved Practice, and better Breeds of Stock, than in the introduction of New Systems—Greatest Change caused by the Prosperity of the Country and the Rise in the Value of Animal Food—vast consequent Increase in the Capital Value of Live-stock and Landed Property ... 16—32

CHAPTER III.

Soil, Climate, and Crops.

Extent of Country and Proportion of various Crops—as influenced by Climate, Situation, and Rainfall—Weight and relative Value of Corn-crops—Examples of Soils of greatest and least natural Fertility—and of an average Soil unmanured and specially manured—Plants which predominate in uncultivated Land ... ... 33—40

CHAPTER IV.

Distribution of Landed Property.

Tendency to Diminution in Number of small Estates—Proportion of Landowners to whole Population as one in a hundred—These, being Heads of Families, equivalent to one in twenty—Hence one-twentieth of Population interested in Landed Property—Increased to one-fifth by the Interests of Tenant-farmers as part Owners of Agricultural Property—One-fifth of the Land held by the Peerage—Not cultivated by Owners but by Farmers—relative Extent of their Holdings in England and in Ireland—Trade and Colonies enable us to dispense with Checks on Increase of Population—That checked in Ireland by Potato Famine—Decrease in Number of smallest Holdings there on return of Prosperity—Diminution of Agricultural Population—and of Yeomen farming their own Land—Experiment of Peasant Proprietors in Ireland ... ... 41—55

CHAPTER V.

Landowner, Farmer, and Labourer.

PAGE

The Landowners, their Position, Duties, and Influence—Their Number, and the immense Capital Value of their Property—The Tenant-farmers, the proportional Extent of their Holdings, their Numbers and Capital—The Labourers—Condition now better than at any previous Period, comparing their Wages with the Price of Bread—Each of the three Classes constantly recruited by Changes of Property and Employment—Result of the System, compared with that of other Countries, shows larger Returns at less Cost—Special Features of System in England—in Scotland—in Ireland—Tenancy-at-will in England—Leases in Scotland—Middlemen in Ireland, and the Result ... ... 56—78

CHAPTER VI.

Land Improvement.

Hindrances by Settlements and Incumbrances—Expedients adopted to overcome the incapacity of Owners to provide Capital for Improvement—State Loans for Land Improvement—Followed by Loans from Land Improvement Companies—

Total Amount so expended—Parliamentary Inquiry into the working of these Loans, and their Results—General Testimony to their remunerative Character—Land Drainage the most remunerative Improvement—Greater Caution required in Expenditure on Buildings—Labourers' Dwellings, judiciously executed and placed, as remunerative as any other Outlay of Landowner's Capital—Better Cottages wanted rather than more of them—Examples of remunerative Expenditure   79—95

CHAPTER VII.

Recent Rise in the Value of Land.

Great Rise in the Value of Land since the Repeal of the Corn Laws—only partly due to the Outlay of Capital in Improvements—Greatest Rise has been in the Grazing Counties, on Grasslands, and in Scotland—The Cause of this—The Scotch Landowner better trained to his Business—Landowning the only Business in which special Training is not usually deemed necessary—Security for Tenant's Capital required—Admirable Principle of Drainage Loans—Extended Powers of Sale in the case of Settled Estates desirable—Settlements should be limited to Lives in being   ...   .   96—110

CHAPTER VIII.

The Government in its Connection with Agriculture.

No Minister of Agriculture, and no Government Control exercised, or State Schools for Agriculture, or Flocks or Herds maintained by Government—The Inclosure Commission the only State Department connected with the Land — Its various Functions—Main Drainage Commissions for Control of Floods—These beneficial where not permitted to remain too long stagnant—Great Engineering Works seldom required—Exchange of Intermixed Lands inexpensive and simple in its Operation—Extent to which the Power of Exchange is used ... ... 111—119

CHAPTER IX.

Waste Lands and Copyholds.

Inclosure of Waste Lands, its Extent and Results—Quality and Occupation of Persons to whom Waste Lands passed—Extent of Public Roads constructed and Value of Lands devoted to Public Objects, at the Cost of the Owners of Common Rights, equal to one-eighth of Value of the whole Land inclosed—Enfranchisement of Copyhold Lands and Buildings—Number completed—Extinction of this objectionable kind of Tenure desirable—Mode of accomplishing this 120—130

CHAPTER X.

Church, Crown, and Charity Estates.

Tithes commuted from Payment in Kind to Money—Unexpected Effect of this in preventing a Rise in the Income of the Church, and increasing that of the Landowners—Parish Clergy a Body of resident Landowners equal in Number to more than one-fourth of those over £200 a year, the removal of whom might prove a Change of great magnitude in its social Effect—Her Majesty's Woods, Forests, and Land Revenues managed with great Judgment—and now yield a net Return to the Exchequer exceeding the Civil List paid to the Queen—General Conditions on which the Farms of the Crown are let—Charity Estates, their Extent and Annual Value—now placed under the general direction of Government—Their Magnitude compared with the Cost of the Civil Administration of the Country ... ... 131—141

CHAPTER XI.

The Future.

Home Production of Bread and Meat limited—Country becoming less of a Farm and more of a Garden—Population, at present Rate of Increase, will in twenty years be forty millions—causing most likely a further Rise in Prices—Prospect of Landowner good—of Tenant-farmer more doubtful—His duty to protect himself by the security of a definite and lengthened Term—Either by Purchase of his Farm or by Lease—Good understandings not likely to resist the increasing Pressure of Competition—Facilities given to Farmers by Government for Purchase in Ireland—if extended to England and Scotland would be more rapidly appropriated—Somehow a definite Term must be secured—Time essential in the Operations of Agriculture—Earl of Leicester's Lease an admirable Example in its principal Features—which admit of Freedom of Management, and provide for Renewal without Exposure to undue Competition—The Labourer, his Work lightened, and Intelligence stimulated, by extended use of Machinery—Cheap Means of Transit, and high Wages of Colonies make him more independent—His political Position likely soon to be improved ... ... 142—156

APPENDIX.

Table showing Rent, Prices, Wages, and Produce in three periods during the last hundred years... 157

	PAGE
Table showing Acreage of Crops and Number of Live-stock in the United Kingdom, in each year since 1867	158
Table showing Quantities and Value of Foreign Grain, and Live-stock, and Provisions imported, in each of the last twenty years	159
Table showing the Annual Yield of Wheat in the United Kingdom, per acre, during each of the last thirty years, and in three periods of ten years each	160

THE LANDED INTEREST.

CHAPTER I.

HOME AND FOREIGN SUPPLY OF FOOD.

One of the most important functions of Government is to take care that there shall be no hindrance to the people supplying themselves with food and clothing, which are the first necessaries of life. And as these are, in one form or another, annual products of the earth, dependent for their abundance on the skill, capital, and labour employed in its cultivation, much of the safety and welfare of a country arises from the condition of its agriculture. That of England has attained an exceptionally high productiveness The best of our land has long been occupied, and, though there is yet much of the inferior class that admits of improvement, it has become our interest as a nation to look also for further supplies from the broader and richer lands of other countries, which, to their advantage and ours, the beneficent principle of Free Trade has placed within our reach.

Value of cereal and animal food imported from abroad.

The progressive increase of foreign supplies during the past twenty years is marvellous, the value of foreign cereal and animal food imported having risen from £35,000,000 in 1857 to £110,000,000 in 1876. The greatest proportional increase has been in the importation of animal food: living animals, fresh and salted meat, fish, poultry, eggs, butter, and cheese, which in that period has risen from an annual value of seven to thirty-six millions sterling. More than half the farinaceous articles imported, other than wheat, are used in the production of beer and spirits.

The imports of animal food during the first fourteen years of Free Trade were comparatively small, the difference of price here and in foreign countries not then affording a margin sufficiently encouraging to justify costly arrangements of transit. But as the price of meat in this country moved steadily up, rising in a few years from fivepence to sevenpence, ninepence, and even a shilling a pound, enterprise with skill and capital were called into rapid action to meet the growing demand. It became clear that an article so valuable could cover the cost of carriage for much longer distances than corn, a pound-weight of meat being many times more valuable than a pound of corn. All kinds of salted meat were expected, and came; but fresh meat (except as live animals), from its perishable nature, was not anticipated in any considerable quantity. The cost of transporting live animals from any great distance must obviously present a very great difficulty. And a further and most serious objection arose, in regard to those from nearer European ports, in the risk of such live animals bringing with them across the seas the contagion of cattle-plague, or other pests, dangerous to the live-stock of this country. All this could be avoided by the importation of fresh meat, and a plan with this object, recently adopted by an American company, has been attended with a large measure of success. The steam-ships in

Rapid rise in value of meat, the comparatively high price of which pays for long transport.

Fresh meat from America may prevent excessive rise of price in Europe.

which the meat is carried have chambers fitted in such a manner that the meat can be kept fresh during the voyage by currents of air cooled by ice. During the last winter and spring large shipments have thus been successfully made, and most of them have arrived in good condition. Should this plan, in addition to the growing importation of live animals, prove safe and successful, we shall have the vast prairies of America added to our own pastures as new sources of supply. This will be a great benefit to the consumers of meat in this country, but probably more by preventing a further rapid rise in the price of meat than by effecting a reduction upon it. The American people are themselves much greater consumers of meat, man for man, than the English, and when prosperity returns to that country, their home consumption will increase, and the surplus for exportation be diminished. Moreover, the English market will take only the best quality. Under any circumstances the English producer has the advantage of at least a penny a pound in the cost and risk of transport against his Transatlantic competitor—an advantage equal to £4 on an average ox. Of this natural advantage nothing can deprive him; and with this he may rest content.

The proportion in which the people of this country are dependent for their principal articles of food on home and foreign supply was the subject of an inquiry by me in 1868, in a paper read to the Statistical Society. At that time I found the foreign supply to be in the proportion of one-fifth of the whole. In the ten years since that time the importation of meat has more than doubled, butter and cheese have risen nearly one-third, wheat more than a third, and other grain has doubled. More than one-fourth of our total consumption of agricultural produce is now obtained from other countries.

<small>Proportion of home and foreign supply of food in the United Kingdom.</small>

But it is a question of interest, both to the home and foreign producer, to ascertain more closely the proportion of the two chief articles, bread and meat. In the past ten years there has been a gradual reduction of the acreage and produce of wheat in this country, and a more than corresponding increase in the foreign supply; the result of which is that we now receive our bread in equal proportions from our own fields and those of the stranger. In regard to meat, and other animal products, ten years ago the proportion of foreign was one-tenth of the whole. It has now risen to nearly one-fourth.

<small>England now chiefly dependent on foreign supply for further increase.</small>

This country thus derives from foreign lands, not only one-half of its bread and nearly one-fourth of its meat and dairy produce, but must also depend on the foreigner for almost the entire addition that may be further required by an increase of its population. In the last ten years there has been no increase in the acreage or production of corn, and little in that of meat. The extent of green crops and grass has slightly increased, from the double impulse of the rise in wages and the increasing demand for dairy produce and meat. But, excluding good lands capable of being rendered fertile by drainage, we appear to have approached a point in agricultural production beyond which capital can be otherwise more profitably expended in this country than in further attempting to force our poorer class of soils. It is cheaper for us as a nation to get the surplus from the richer lands of America and Southern Russia, where the virgin soil is still unexhausted; or from the more ancient agriculture of India, which, with its cheap and abundant labour more skilfully applied, and its means of transport extended and better utilised, seems destined to become one of the principal sources of our future supply of corn.

The cost of carriage depends very much on distance, and as the chief supply of wheat comes from great distances—California, the Black Sea, and India—the cost of transporting a quantity equal to the produce of an acre in England is seldom less, and often more, than 40s. Hay and straw are so bulky that they can only bear the cost of carriage from near Continental ports. Fresh meat from America, from the costly methods necessary to preserve it, will, on the produce of an acre, cost equal to 40s. for transport to this country. This natural protection enjoyed by the British farmer in his proximity to the home market, as compared with the foreign farmer who seeks our market for his produce, thus

Cost of carriage equal to the rent of land in England.

gives him an advantage equal to the present average rent of his land, and forms some reasonable compensation for the higher taxes and wages which he has to pay as compared with his competitors in most foreign countries.

<small>Agricultural statistics of the United Kingdom.</small>

The total home produce can now be very correctly calculated from the annual agricultural returns. The collection of these returns was instituted in Ireland at the time of the potato famine in 1847, and they have been published continuously since that time. The information is collected by the constabulary, a semi-military force, stationed in all parts of the country, and is arranged by the Registrar-General, and annually printed.

Not for twenty years afterwards were there any complete returns from Great Britain. After long perseverance I succeeded in obtaining a Resolution of the House of Commons in favour of the collection of agricultural statistics, which was in consequence carried out for the first time in 1867, the collection of the returns being made by the officers of the Inland Revenue, and their arrangement for publication by the Statistical Department of the Board of Trade. The experience gained by ten years' repetition of the various inquiries has created such a fund of local knowledge among the officers of the Inland Revenue that there can now be no 'doubt entertained of the substantial accuracy of the returns. Minute accuracy is not expected or required, but the comparisons from year to year show the relative accuracy obtained to be sufficient for all practical purposes. *Their accuracy sufficient for practical use.*

It appears from these returns that though there was an exceptional decrease in the acreage of wheat in 1876, arising from the great floods in the autumn seed-time of 1875, which prevented a considerable proportion of the land being sown, no great change has occurred during the past ten years in the production of wheat in Great Britain. It has somewhat diminished in England, and largely in Ireland, but the diminution is quite made up by a corresponding increase in barley. Oats remain much the same, and the total extent of arable is very slightly altered. *Their main features.*

Increase of pasture.

The permanent pasture during the same period has increased 8 per cent., no doubt from the increased cost of labour and the gradual rise in the value of live-stock and its produce. This increase of 8 per cent., amounting to nearly one million acres, not having diminished the extent of corn, must represent an addition of that breadth gained by reclamation during the ten years; and, as some considerable extent of land is yearly taken from cultivation by the increase of towns and the construction of new railroads, this shows an important gain by agricultural enterprise.

The general extent of green crops has very slightly altered in the ten years, potatoes alone *Increase of* showing some diminution. A large increase, *the mangold crop.* however, in the proportion of mangold is shown by a rise of 100,000 acres more than in 1867. This is a root-crop peculiarly well suited to the deep soils and dry and warm climate of the south-east and southern counties; and its keeping properties, continuing well into the following summer, are a great recommendation to the stock farmer. A rise of 40 per cent. in the breadth cultivated, within so short a period as ten years, is a convincing proof that the great value of this plant is at length beginning to be generally recognised, and there seems a probability of its continued extension. In live-stock there has been a moderate increase in Great Britain during the past ten years.

In Ireland the change of crops has been greater than in England or Scotland, the extent of land under corn having diminished in ten years by 12 per cent. Wheat has fallen to less than one-half, there is an increase of 28 per cent. in barley, but a decrease of nearly 10 per cent. in oats. Potatoes have fallen 12 per cent., while turnips have slightly increased. On the whole there has been a diminution of 267,000 acres of land under corn, and an addition of 203,000 acres to permanent meadow and grass. The reduction of the acreage of wheat, for which the climate of most parts of Ireland is too moist, and the considerable decline in potatoes, the tempting but precarious crop upon which that country has hitherto too much relied, are evident signs of prudence and prosperity. In the same *margin:* Diminution of corn and increase of grass in Ireland.

period, though there has been a reduction in the number of sheep, that is much more than compensated by an increase in cattle. And as the expenditure on drainage and land improvement, and in the building of farm-houses and labourers' cottages, has been greatly increasing, year by year, the state of agriculture in Ireland, chiefly owing to the high price of live-stock, and the increasing demand for store animals to be fattened in Great Britain, now appears to have attained a position of general progress and prosperity greater than has ever been previously experienced in that portion of the United Kingdom.

<small>Present great agricultural prosperity of that country.</small>

The extent of land under the various crops in the United Kingdom in 1877 was, in wheat, 3,321,000 acres; barley, 2,652,000 acres; oats, 4,239,000 acres; potatoes, 1,393,000 acres; other green crops, 3,566,000 acres; flax, 130,000 acres; hops, 70,000 acres; bare fallow, 633,000 acres; grass under rotation, 6,441,000 acres; permanent pasture, 24,000,000 acres (besides mountain pastures and wastes); woods and plantations, 2,511,000.

The number of live-stock of various kinds in 1877 was, of horses, 2,834,000; cattle, 9,693,000; sheep, 32,157,000; pigs, 3,964,000.

By the aid of the agricultural returns, and those of the annual imports of foreign and colonial produce, I have constructed the following Table, showing the comparative quantities of home and foreign growth, and the value of agricultural produce at present required for the annual consumption of the people and live-stock of this country. The grass, green crops other than potatoes, and hay used on the farm, and straw, are not included, nor the value of the increase of horses.

The total value of the home crop is considerably more than double that which we import, but the proportion of vegetable and animal food is singularly close, as will be seen by this further arrangement of the figures:—

Quantity and value of home and foreign agricultural produce, respectively, consumed annually in the British Islands.

	Home Growth.	Foreign.
Value of corn and vegetable produce	£125,737,500	£52,537,500
Value of animal produce	135,000,000	58,170,000

Table showing Comparative Quantity and Value of Home and Foreign Agricultural Produce consumed Annually.

	Home Growth.	Foreign Growth.	Total.	Value of Home Growth.	Value of Foreign.	Total Value.
	Cwts.	Cwts.	Cwts.	£	£	£
Wheat	55,000,000	55,000,000	110,000,000	32,187,500	32,187,500	64,375,000
Barley	44,000,000	11,000,000	55,000,000	19,800,000	4,950,000	24,750,000
Oats	64,000,000	12,000,000	76,000,000	28,800,000	5,400,000	34,200,000
Beans and Peas	14,000,000	5,000,000	19,000,000	6,300,000	2,250,000	8,550,000
Ind. an Corn	...	20,000,000	20,000,000	...	7,000,000	7,000,000
Total Corn	177,000,000	103,000,000	280,000,000	£87,087,500	£51,787,500	£138,875,000
Potatoes	111,000,000	5,000,000	116,000,000	16,650,000	750,000	17,400,000
Wool	1,214,000	3,160,000	4,374,000	8,500,000	22,120,000	30,620,000
Butchers' Meat, Bacon, Hams, and Pork	24,500,000	6,300,000	30,800,000	87,000,000	22,050,000	109,050,000
Cheese and Butter	3,000,000	3,100,000	6,100,000	13,500,000	14,000,000	27,500,000
Milk	...	...	...	26,000,000	...	26,000,000
Hay for Horses, agricultural and not agricultural	80,000,000	...	80,000,000	16,000,000	...	16,000,000
Straw sold for Town Consumption	40,000,000	...	40,000,000	6,000,000	...	6,000,000
Total	436,714,000	120,560,000	557,274,000	£260,737,500	£110,707,500	£371,445,000

The quantity of Indian corn imported in 1876 was nearly 40,000,000 cwt., an amount hitherto exceptional and unprecedented, and therefore not included in its full amount in the preceding estimate.

CHAPTER II.

CHANGES AND PROGRESS OF AGRICULTURE IN RECENT YEARS.

The most striking features of recent agricultural progress.

BEFORE entering on a more detailed description of the principles which regulate the agriculture and general management of landed property in this country, it may be useful shortly to notice its more recent progress, and those changes of practice which science or art, or the circumstances of his position in regard to competition or labour, have forced on the British farmer. With a few exceptions the change will be found rather in the more general diffusion of a knowledge of good principles and practice than in any considerable advance upon either.

The reaping and mowing machines.

The most striking feature of agricultural progress within the last twenty years has been the general introduction of reaping-machines, one of which can do the work of ten men. This has multiplied the effect of human labour tenfold, and that at the most critical season, the harvest, when the entire crop ripens within a fortnight, and must with all possible expedition be saved without loss of time. For hay-making, a similar machine is in the same proportion available. It would be difficult to reckon the vast saving which the introduction of this most important invention has made at these most critical periods, haytime and harvest.

Next to it is the steam-plough, which, on heavy land and in large fields, especially where coal is moderate in cost, and water easily available, is both economical and expeditious. A steam-plough, capable of ploughing ten acres a day, will do the labour of ten men and twenty horses, and, where deep culture is advantageous, will execute the work much more effectively, and with no injurious trampling of the tender soil. But it is as yet a costly implement, beyond the reach of small farmers except when hired as an auxiliary, and not capable of doing its work with economy within small *The steam-plough.*

enclosures. The saving of labour is great in suitable localities, but it is not so uniformly applicable, nor does it so certainly and quickly repay its cost as the reaping-machine. On light and friable soils the double-furrow plough, balancing itself with greatly less friction in proportion than the single plough, is found to do the same work with one man and three horses as two single ploughs with two men and four horses. This is equal to a saving of 50 per cent. in man-power, and 25 per cent. in horse-power, and it will become more generally available on the lighter soils if any serious pressure arises from scarcity of labour. In the threshing of corn, and cutting of straw and hay for fodder, and the grinding and bruising of corn and cake for horse and cattle food, the aid of steam-power has long been used by the farmers of this country.

The double-furrow plough.

General use of steam-power in manipulation of crops.

Successive corn-crops.

Next to the economy of labour may be ranked the increase of produce by the expedient of taking two corn-crops in succession where the land is clean and in high condition, and can bear the application of special manure, and where the agriculturist is free to follow a rational system of farming. The four-course system of alternate corn and green crops—wheat, turnips, barley, clover—had two great advantages, first, by alternating restorative and cleansing crops with corn; and second, by regular distribution of labour throughout the year. The introduction of guano, nitrate of soda, and other ammoniacal and phosphatic manures, has now rendered the farmer comparatively independent of this alternate system of cropping. As the supply of nitrate is believed to be capable of lasting for a very long period, we may reckon with considerable certainty on its continuance at a moderate price. It might become an instrument of great national value if any unforeseen occurrence should cut off one of our main supplies of wheat, that of Russia, for example. If only the twentieth part of the corn land of the United Kingdom were called on to bear an additional wheat-crop, the loss would be at once made good, and with no perceptible strain on our agricultural system. If all Europe were shut against us, we should be quickly able

Use to which this might be put in time of war.

to meet the increased home demand by double-cropping to the extent of one-tenth of our corn-land, and without any greater change in the demand for nitrate of soda than has already been met by the advancing supplies of recent years. It is unnecessary to consider the position of this country were even a heavier calamity to befall us, obtaining as we do from the foreigner so large a proportion of our food, for it is not conceivable that the producers of corn in any country would desire to see the best market in the world long closed to them. But it is clear that we possess in this power of taking a second crop of wheat a latent reserve force which might, on very short notice, be brought into action, and which should dispel all fear of our being starved into submission in case of war; and this without reckoning anything on the immense reserve power of cereal production which is stored up in the pasture-lands, ready in case of need.

Likely to check a permanent rise in the price of wheat.

It is a power, moreover, that will check any considerable permanent rise in the price of wheat. A decline in the acreage under wheat, when not caused by a bad seed-time, is the natural result of low price; but when the price rises, increased acreage quickly follows. Were the price to rise steadily, and show signs of permanence, the second-crop system would extend, and continue to do so until the increase of produce was found to check the rise in price. Barley may be taken after barley with more success on many soils than wheat; and where there is reason to suppose that a second crop of wheat, however carefully the ground may have been managed and manured, may be likely to fail, barley may, with great probability, be expected to succeed.

The use of nitrate of soda or other sources of ammonia, combined with phosphatic manures, promises to be a more permanent resource to British agriculture than Peruvian guano, which unites the same properties in itself, but seems likely soon to become exhausted. Autumn culture, aided by the command of time which steam-power has given to the agriculturist, and that supplemented by spring top-dressings of nitrates and phosphates, have made continuous corn-cropping possible and profit-

Autumn culture and steam-power, with imported manures, have given great command of crops.

able, without injury to the land, whenever soil and circumstances render such a practice necessary. The old plan of relying on the resources of the farm by depending on the manure made upon it, while the corn and meat were sold away, will not answer now. Commerce and mercantile enterprise have provided other means for maintaining fertility at a cheaper cost, and in a more commodious and portable form. One cwt. of nitrate of soda will give a more certain return of corn than fifty times its weight in farmyard-manure, and can be carried to and spread upon the ground at one-fiftieth of the labour. The proof of this, in Mr. Lawes' experiments, has been before the country for more than thirty years, and yet it is only beginning to be generally recognised.

Great value to British agriculture of Mr. Lawes' experiments.

To Mr. J. B. Lawes the agriculture of this country is more indebted than to any other living man. For thirty-three years he has conducted, at his own cost, a series of experiments on his estate in Hertfordshire, the results of which have been annually published, and the farm itself, with every detail of the work, has been laid open to public inspection and criticism. Among other valuable results, one most useful fact has been elicited, that of that mass of dark, strongly-smelling substance called dung, its sole property as a manure depends upon the small quantity of chemical salts and of organic nitrogen which it contains, the bulky organic matter being only useful in making the land work better, and rendering it more capable of absorbing and retaining moisture. Beginning in 1844 with wheat, the staff of life in this country, he for eight years concentrated his attention upon it, dividing his experimental field into twenty-two plots, upon two of which no manure has ever been applied, and upon the other twenty a carefully considered variety of manures has been continuously used. In 1852 he commenced a similar series of experiments with barley, and in 1869 on a smaller area with oats. Experiments with leguminous crops had been for a series of years continued, but this species of plant being found, when grown too frequently on the same land, to be peculiarly subject to disease, which no conditions of manuring appeared capable of obviating, they were discontinued. With regard to red clover, when the land becomes clover-sick, it was found that no manure could be relied on to secure a crop, and continuous crops of it are therefore impossible. Experiments on the various root-crops were continued for series of years, and the result published; also on sugar-beet; and in 1876 a commencement was made with potatoes. His experiments on the corn-crops go on without cessation. In 1856 an important series of experiments was commenced on grass-land, which, with very little change on each of the twenty plots, has been continued to the present time. The average of the past twenty years shows that the natural produce may be doubled, and even trebled, by the continuous use of special manures. Seeing that nearly two-thirds of the cultivated area of this country, and all the uncultivated, are in grass, this series of experiments is of very great interest and value. After thirty-three successive wheat-crops it is not surprising that the soil begins to exhibit symptoms of exhaustion. The rotation experiments

Some of their special lessons.

show that this may be corrected by interposing a heavily dunged green crop, such as mangold, while the introduction of red clover between the corn-crops is also found to add greatly to the corn-producing power of the soil. To attain a maximum paying produce, he finds that the land should be dunged heavily for mangold, to be followed with wheat, or barley, or oats, according to soil and climate, for several years in succession; then interpose clover, and follow it with corn-crops, keeping the land perfectly clean, and manuring all the corn-crops with nitrate of soda and superphosphate. When the land shows need of change, begin again with heavily dunged green crops. Successive crops of barley he finds to pay better, and are more certain than either wheat or oats, and give more corn in proportion to straw. If a heavily dunged green crop is occasionally introduced, it is not necessary to give any other manure to the corn-crops than nitrate of soda and superphosphate. Potash (which may be supplied by dung) is very necessary in a grass-manure, especially for clover, which, unlike corn, is injured by ammonia. The grass experiments show that by giving food to the plants, the strongest and best varieties appropriate what they most need, and, by the law of the strongest, put the weakest down. In the best plots the weeds almost disappear, while on one plot, to which no manure is applied, the weeds form 50 per cent. of the produce. Besides these experiments on crops, Mr. Lawes has carried out investigations on the feeding of live-stock, and on the different values of their food, both as affecting the processes of fattening and the quality and value of the manure.

The Woburn experiments.

The Royal Agricultural Society has commenced a series of experiments on the growth of crops and the fattening of live-stock, with a special relation to the manures applied and the food used, and to the effect of the manures resulting from specific kinds of food. The Duke of Bedford, with great liberality and public spirit, has undertaken the cost of these experiments, and has placed suitable land and buildings at the disposal of the Society, whose Council, under the guidance of Mr. Lawes,*

---

* To the general regret Mr. Lawes has retired from this duty.

General Progress of Improvement.

and of Dr. Voelcker, their consulting chemist, regulate and superintend them. They are open to public inspection, and under such management the most useful results may be anticipated.

There has been a great extension of drainage in recent years, and in the construction of improved farm-buildings, and in the better lodging of farm-labourers in more commodious cottages. And in regard to live-stock there has been a wider diffusion of the best breeds, and generally an earlier maturity obtained in the process of fattening. The use of improved implements and machinery has greatly extended, as also has the general application of locomotive steam-power to the threshing and other preparation of crops for market or feeding purposes. Cheap descriptions of corn are largely employed in the fattening of stock, and also oil-cake, cotton-cake, and rape-cake. For these, and for bones, guano, and nitrate of soda used as manure, the annual expenditure cannot now be less than twelve millions sterling.

Extension of land drainage, and improvement of farm labourers' cottages, and housing for live-stock.

Large annual expenditure on cattle food and portable manure.

The change in the last thirty years more in the general diffusion of improved practices, and better live-stock, than in the introduction of new systems.

But, with the exception of the reaping-machine and steam-plough, and the more general use of steam-power, and other implements and machines, there is really little that is new in the practice of the last quarter of a century. The present system of drainage was previously well understood. Bones, guano, and nitrate of soda were fully appreciated by those who then used them. Covered buildings and autumn cultivation had been introduced. Mr. Hudson, of Castleacre, in Norfolk, then manured his land for every crop. In running my eye over the account which I wrote of English agriculture in 1850, I find descriptions of good farming in nearly every part of the country, the details of which differ very little from the practice of the present day. Mr. Pusey and Sir John Conroy in Berkshire; Mr. Thomas in Bedfordshire; Mr. Beasley in Northampton; Mr. Paget in Notts; Mr. Torr in Lincoln; Mr. Mechi, Mr. Fisher Hobbs, and Mr. Hutley, in Essex; Mr. Huxtable in Dorset; Jonas Webb in Cambridgeshire; Mr. Morton in Gloucestershire; the Messrs. Wells and Outhwaite in Yorkshire; Mr. Fleming of Barrochan, Mr. M'Culloch of Auchness, and Mr. George Hope, in Scotland; Lord Lucan, Mr. St. John Jeffryes, and Mr. Boyd, of Castlewellan, in Ireland, and many others, then carried out the business of farming in a manner that would bear favourable comparison with the prize-farms of the present year. And, as to breeds of cattle and sheep, the brothers Colling's and Messrs. Booth's and Mr. Bates's Shorthorns; George Turner's and the Messrs. Quartley's Devons; Mr. Bakewell's Leicesters; Jonas Webb's Southdowns—are not surpassed by the best of the present day. The change has been not in any considerable progress beyond what was then the best, but in a general upheaval of the middling and the worst towards the higher platform then occupied by the few.

Towards this end, but beyond all efforts of the agriculturists themselves, or of the engineers and chemists who have done so much to aid them in developing the capabilities of the land, has been the influence of the general prosperity and growing trade and wealth of the country. Thirty years ago, probably not more

Influence upon agriculture of the general prosperity of the country in the rise of the price of meat, and the consequent increase in

than one-third of the people of this country consumed animal food more than once a week. Now, nearly all of them eat it, in meat, or cheese, or butter, once a day. This has more than doubled the average consumption per head; and when the increase of population is considered, has probably trebled the total consumption of animal food in this country. The increased supply has come partly from our own fields, but chiefly from abroad. The leap which the consumption of meat took in consequence of the general rise of wages in all branches of trade and employment, could not have been met without foreign supplies, and these could not have been secured except by such a rise of price as fully paid the risk and cost of transport. The additional price on the home-produce was all profit to the landed interests of this country, and is now being shared among them, partly in rise of rent, partly in increase of profit, and chiefly in rise of wages and expenses, and local rates. Within the last twenty-five years, the capital value of the live-stock of the United Kingdom has risen from one hundred and forty-six to two hundred and sixty millions sterling, a gain of one hundred and fourteen millions.

It will be subsequently shown, when treating of the value of land, that within a somewhat shorter period the increase of the land-rent of this country, when capitalised at thirty years' purchase, shows an increased value of three hundred and thirty-one millions sterling. When we add to this the increase of farm-capital, through the rise in the value of live-stock, one hundred and fourteen millions, there is the amazing sum of four hundred and forty-five millions sterling as the gain to the agriculturists—the landowners and farmers—and, in higher wages, to the agricultural labourers of the United Kingdom, from the improvement of land and the general prosperity of the country. I may, perhaps, be excused for quoting the concluding words of my volume, written in 1851, at a time of great agricultural depression, when I stated that I believed the landlords and tenants of England possessed energy and capacity sufficient to meet and adapt themselves to the Free Trade policy, "which, in its extraordinary effect on the welfare of all other classes of the community, would, sooner or later, bear good fruits also to them."

CHAPTER III.

SOIL, CLIMATE, AND CROPS.

THE total extent of the United Kingdom is 76,300,000 acres, of which 26,300,000 are in mountain pasture and waste, and 50,000,000 in crops, meadows, permanent pasture, and woods and forests. Of the crops, one-fourth is in various kinds of corn, one-eighth in green crops, one-eighth in grass under rotation, and one-half in meadows and permanent pasture. About a thirtieth of the whole surface of the kingdom is in woods and forests. These proportions show the prevailing system of husbandry, and reveal the cause of its increasing productiveness. Three-fourths of the whole are green crops, which feed and clean, or grass, which rests and maintains the remaining fourth in corn. This preponderance of restorative over exhaustive crops greatly exceeds that of any

[marginal note: Extent of the country and proportions of various crops.]

other country, and is very much due to the climate.

<small>as influenced by climate,</small> The climate of the eastern side is drier than that of the west, the fall of rain at equal altitudes being as 25 inches in the east to 35 in the west. The drought and heat are greatest in the east, centre, and south-east in spring and summer. The whole western side of the country is comparatively mild and moist, and specially adapted for green crops and pasture. The east, having generally a deeper soil and greater heat in summer, is best suited to wheat and barley. It produces 64 per cent. of all the wheat and barley grown, and 74 per cent. of the pulse-crops. The west, on the other hand, contains more than twice the extent of permanent pasture, and produces nearly double the number of cattle. The waters of the Gulf Stream envelop the British Islands. Their vapours, carried over every part of the kingdom by prevailing west winds, temper the cold of winter and the heats of summer. This favours the growth, on the west especially, of succulent herbage and green crops, and we are free from the extremes

experienced on the Continent. Grass and green crops flourish in all parts of the country, and both in the low lands and on the mountain pastures of the west and north, sheep feed unsheltered and unhoused during both winter and summer. Beasts of prey are unknown.

The annual rainfall in the lower parts of the country varies from 25 to 35 inches. In the mountainous districts these figures may be doubled. But, limiting our consideration to the cultivated lands, it must be obvious that an annual rainfall upon an acre of land, in the one case of 2,500 tons and in the other of 3,500 tons, accompanied by corresponding humidity of atmosphere, will greatly modify the respective systems of husbandry practised. Accordingly, the eastern half of the country may be correctly described as the corn and fattening region, and the western half as the dairy and breeding region of the kingdom. The winter temperature is more severe in the east than the west, and that of the summer warmer and more sunny, and better suited to the ripening of wheat;

and rainfall.

while that of the west, being less scorching and more cloudy, is better adapted to pasture and oats. The value of live-stock is so much greater than corn, that it is not found profitable to push the limit of cultivation to a greater height than 800 feet in the east and 500 in the west, and these limits are becoming more circumscribed by the increasing cost of labour and the continued rise in the value of live-stock.

Weight and relative value of corn-crops. The soil varies greatly in fertility, and its cultivation is regulated both by the amount it yields and the cost of cultivating it. The most profitable and productive soil is that which is at once fertile and easy of cultivation. A rich loam which yields a ton of wheat to the acre is less costly in labour than a poor clay which yields little more than half that weight. Between corn and straw an average crop of wheat, barley, and oats, will weigh two tons an acre; about two-fifths being corn and three-fifths straw, though the proportion of straw to corn in wheat and oats is greater than in barley. A ton of wheat, at the average price of the last fifteen years, is worth £11 14s.; a ton of barley,

£9 12s.; and of oats, £9. But the wheat is more costly to grow, as it is four months longer in the soil, and therefore takes more out of it than either barley or oats, and requires either a better soil or more enriching preparation. On soils of equal quality the average weight of barley and oats yielded by an acre exceeds that of wheat in about the same proportion as it falls short of it in value per ton. Hence, where the soil and climate are equally suited to the production of these varieties of corn, the choice of one or the other is more a question of convenience than profit, and depends much on the local value of the different kinds of straw.

The fertility of a soil may be expressed by examples taken, 1st, in the natural state of pasture, and 2nd, on similar soils after treatment. The maximum of fertility in the natural state is a rich pasture capable of fattening an ox and two sheep on an acre. Such soils are exceptional, though in most counties they are to be met with. The Pawlet Hams in Somersetshire, for example, is a tract of rich alluvial

Examples of soils of the greatest and least natural fertility,

soil on the River Parrott, stretching along the sea-board. It is in permanent pasture, and is let for grazing at £5 to £6 of rent an acre. Some of the marsh-lands of Sussex and Kent are of equal fertility. And on certain limestone lands, not alluvial, in various parts of the country, both east and west, feeding pastures of great fertility are met with. Such lands, as they require neither labour nor manure, yield the largest rents to their owners. The profit to the stock-feeder beyond the rent paid to the landowner depends on the skill with which he conducts his business. The minimum of fertility may be exemplified by a bleak mountain pasture, where ten acres will barely maintain a small sheep.

and of an average soil unmanured, and specially manured.

The artificial maximum and minimum of fertility which result from the treatment of soils of the same quality is more instructive, and may be clearly exemplified by taking two of the experiments which have been carried on by Mr. Lawes of Rothamsted, in Hertfordshire, for the last thirty years. Confining the comparison to the average of the last twelve years, the following is the weight in pounds of an average crop :—

	Corn.	Straw.	Total.
	lbs.	lbs.	lbs.
1st. Wheat grown continuously, without manure	730	1,120	1,850
2nd. Wheat grown continuously, with special manure	2,342	4,928	7,270

The soils here are exactly similar and in the same field, strong land on clay with a substratum of chalk; the management is the same, in so far as culture is concerned; both crops are kept equally clean and free from weeds, the same seed is used, and they are exposed to the same changes of weather. The only difference is, that in the one case nature has for thirty years been unassisted by manure, and in the other the soil receives every year the various kinds of manure which have been found most suitable to the crop. The result of this treatment is a return of three times the weight of corn and four times the weight of straw, for an expenditure in manure which leaves a profit of 100 per cent. on its cost. In both cases the wheat is grown continuously year after year.

The plants which predominate in uncultivated land depend both on the nature of the soil and on the climate and situation. On poor gravel, furze grows in abundance; on peaty uplands, short heath; on cold, wet-bottomed soils, rushes cover the ground. Natural woods of birch and oak are found in sheltered Highland glens, and self-sown Scotch firs spread themselves in the neighbourhood of extensive pine forests.

CHAPTER IV.

DISTRIBUTION OF LANDED PROPERTY.

THE distribution of landed property in England, so far as ownership is concerned, is, by the growing wealth of the country, constantly tending to a reduction in the number of small estates. This tendency is further promoted by the law, which permits entails and settlements, thus hindering the natural sale of land so dealt with; and also by rights of primogeniture, which prevent subdivision of landed property among the family in case of intestacy. Cultivation thus passes out of the hands of small owners into those of tenant-farmers, causing a gradual decrease of the agricultural population, and a proportionate increase of the towns. This has been much accelerated by a policy of Free Trade, which has at once opened up the markets of the world for our commerce, and for the

Tendency of landed property to diminution in the number of small estates.

produce of our mines and manufactures. These are advantageously interchanged for the corn and other agricultural products of foreign lands. This will go on while the commerce is found mutually profitable. And it will be profitable so long as, by superior skill and enterprise, combined with exceptional mineral advantages, we can undersell other countries in the produce of our manufactories and mines, while they can supply us with corn at a cheaper rate than we can grow it at home. Our present relation with foreign countries is becoming like that of a crowded capital, which draws its fresh supplies of vegetables, milk, and meat, from the market-gardens, meadows, and rich grazings in its vicinity, but looks to more distant lands for the corn and other commodities which bear long transport from cheaper and more distant farms. More than one-half of our corn is now of foreign growth, and nearly one-fourth of our meat and dairy produce; whilst year by year our corn-land is giving place to the more profitable produce afforded by the milk and grazing and market-garden farms, which are gradually extending their circle. Such produce renders the land more valuable, more tempting prices are offered for it to the small landowners, and their numbers decrease. Wealthy men from the mines and manufactories and shipping and colonial interests, and the learned professions, desire to become proprietors of land; and some competition exists between them and those landowners whose increasing wealth tempts them on suitable opportunities to enlarge the boundaries of their domains. Thus small proprietors are bought out, and agricultural landowners diminish in number; while, side by side with them, vast urban populations are growing up, having little other connection with the land than that of affording the best market for its produce.

The Domesday Book for the United Kingdom, lately published, divides the landowners into two classes—those who have less than one acre of land, and those who have one acre and upwards. The former comprise 70 per cent. of the whole; but as none of this class has so much as an acre, and they hold together less than a two-hundredth part of the land, they may

Proportion of landowners to whole population, 320,000 to 33,000,000

be regarded as householders only. Excluding these as not properly agricultural landowners, it may then fairly be said that one person in every hundred of the entire population is a landowner. Subdividing that figure by the average numbers of each family, it may be concluded that every twentieth head of a family is an owner of land.

<small>Increased by the interests of tenant-farmers as part owners of agricultural property.</small>

But the tenant-farmers are entitled also to be reckoned as part owners of agricultural property, for in the crops and live and dead stock they own equal to one-fifth of the whole capital value of the land. Part of this is incorporated with the soil, and it is all as indispensable for the production of crops as the land itself. As cultivators, they employ and possess individually a larger capital than the peasant proprietors of other countries in their double capacity as owners and cultivators. They are 1,160,000 in number, and when added to 320,000 owners of one acre and upwards, make 1,480,000 altogether, engaged in the ownership and cultivation of the soil. When reckoned as heads of families they comprise more than one-fifth of the total male adult population; and it is thence not unreasonable to infer that, in that proportion, the people of this country are more or less interested in the preservation of landed property.

When we come more closely to analyse the landowning class, the aggregation of land amongst small numbers becomes very conspicuous. One-fourth of the whole territory, excluding those under one acre, is held by 1,200 persons, at an average for each of 16,200 acres; another fourth by 6,200 persons, at an average for each of 3,150 acres; another fourth by 50,770 persons, at an average for each of 380 acres; whilst the remaining fourth is held by 261,830 persons, at an average for each of 70 acres. An interesting compilation from the Domesday Books by the *Scotsman* newspaper, shows that the Peerage of the United Kingdom, about 600 in number, possess among them rather more than a fifth of all the land, and between a tenth and an eleventh of its annual income. {One-fifth of the land held by the Peerage.}

The great bulk of the land in the United Kingdom is not cultivated by the owners, but by tenant-occupiers. Of these there are 561,000 {Not cultivated by owners but by tenant-farmers;}

in Great Britain, and 600,000 in Ireland. Excluding the mountains, wastes, and water, the cultivated land is held by these at an average of 56 acres each in Great Britain, and 26 acres in Ireland. But the proportion of large and small farms in the two countries is very different, nearly half the land in Ireland being held in small farms under 15 acres each, while less than a fifth of Great Britain is so occupied. 86 per cent. of the farmers in Ireland hold nearly half the land, while 70 per cent. in Great Britain hold less than a fifth. Agriculture is the principal occupation of the people of Ireland, the revenue from the land there forming twice as much as that from all other sources, whilst in Great Britain it is but a seventh of the whole. Hence in Ireland the possession and occupancy of land is the great political question, while in Great Britain it has ceased to have prominence.

This country, from its insular position and the great resources it possesses in minerals of iron and coal, and the outlet it finds in extensive colonies, has advantages which have hitherto enabled it to disregard those prudential considerations which, in some other countries, have checked the rapid increase of population. Where full employment and the means of subsistence are abundant, population increases in geometrical progression, and therefore in a far more rapid proportion than the increased productiveness of the soil, which, after a certain point, is stationary. The population of England increases more rapidly than that of France, because our enormous foreign trade, amounting in value to £20 per head of our population, enables us to add the food resources of other countries to our own. Our surplus population, not wedded to the soil by property, emigrate to countries of the same language, at the rate of 100,000 a year; partly to the United States, and partly to our own colonies. Our agriculture is no longer influenced by considerations of the means of finding employment for surplus labour, but is now being developed on the principle of obtaining the largest produce at the least cost, the same principle by which the power-loom has supplanted the hand-loom. In this process many ancient ties are loosened, and among them that adhesiveness to the soil which for generations has more bound the English labourer than the owner of the land to the parish of his birth; the man of most ancient known descent being in very many cases the labourer. The process is a wholesome one so long as the command to multiply and replenish the earth has not been fulfilled. And the general rise of wages among the labouring classes both in town and country, with the diminution of pauperism, in the last five years, would seem to be a satisfactory proof that there is still room in this country, and no need to check the growth of population.

<small>Checked in Ireland, by potato famine in 1846. Its results.</small>

Such a check, however, took place in Ireland at the time of the potato famine in 1846. The population was then eight millions and a half. Within five years it had fallen to six millions and a half, nearly one-fourth of the people having either emigrated or died. The deaths from fever and famine had ceased in 1850, but the emigration continued, partly to Great Britain and the colonies, but chiefly to the United States. The population had fallen in

1871 to 5,412,000, and was then almost the same as that of 1801, seventy years before. There is no darker page than this in the history of our country in the present or preceding century. Millions of money were lavishly spent by the Government in direct relief, and in relief and improvement works to give employment, with a view to palliate the collapse which befell a people who had no resources when the potato failed them. The landowners in the more distressed districts were nearly as much broken down as their tenants. They had either encouraged or not discouraged the continued subdivision of small farms, as well as the rapid increase of the people, by which, so long as the potato could be relied on, their rents were increased. The famine-stricken land was everywhere abandoned by the starving occupiers, and thrown tenantless upon the owners' hands, making many of them bankrupt. An 'Encumbered Estates Act' was passed, to sell off the lands of those proprietors whose incumbrances had overwhelmed them, and substitute others more capable of fulfilling the duties of landowners. In a few years land to the value of twenty-five millions sterling was disposed of, twenty-four of which were distributed among creditors. In order to secure the landowners' prompt attention in future to the condition of the people, the incidence of the poor-rates, which had previously been placed wholly on the tenant-occupier, was divided equally between him and the landowner. In fifteen years, emigration and the sale of encumbered estates had removed the most needy class of the population. Prosperity then began again to dawn upon agriculture in Ireland, works of improvement followed the introduction of capital, supplied partly by Government loans and partly by the new landowners. Labour having become less plentiful, was better employed and more liberally paid, and the more energetic of the small farmers were ready to enlarge their holdings on every favourable opportunity. As time went on, a great change was found to have taken place, the old eagerness for the occupancy of land returned, but not for its subdivision. In less than thirty years, 270,000 of the smallest holdings were merged

Decrease of smallest holdings

into adjoining larger farms, one-half of the small holdings of 1845 having totally disappeared. The tide of emigration began to turn, extreme poverty ceased, the proportion of paupers to the population became much lower, and the costs of poor relief nearly one-half less, than in either England or Scotland. This was accompanied by better wages to the labourer, higher profits to the farmer, and a rise in the value of land, all fostered by a growing demand for the kind of produce which the soil and climate of Ireland are specially adapted to yield. But the lesson left by the previous disaster has led to the gravest distrust in the system of very small holdings, in a country producing neither wine nor oil, and where the occupier is not the owner of the land.

on the return of prosperity in Ireland.

It is worthy of note that the strictly rural parishes of England exhibit some decline of population. In one-fourth of the registration districts there has been a diminution of the agricultural population in the ten years ending 1871, amounting altogether to 108,000. And it is quite certain that this continues. It arises from

Diminution of agricultural population in proportion to other classes in England.

the natural draft to the better-paid labour of the mining, manufacturing, and other industrial centres, which are augmented both by this immigration and by natural increase. Diminished population in the rural districts is followed by a rise of wages; and this leads to greater economy of labour, both by the introduction of labour-saving machinery and the conversion of arable land to pasture, where the nature of the soil admits. The higher price of meat and dairy-produce also contributes to this change. But the loss in numbers of the agricultural districts is amply made good by the gain in the rest of the country, the population now employed in agriculture being small compared with that of the other industries. Fifty years ago a fifth of the working population of England was engaged in agriculture. At the present time there is less than a tenth.

<small>Class of yeomen, farming their own land, now in very small proportion to that of</small>

The land of the United Kingdom may be said to be now almost wholly cultivated by tenant-farmers. The class of yeomen, or small landowners farming their own land, is found here and there in England, but scarcely at all in Scotland, and now bears but small proportion to the whole. Many of the larger landowners retain a farm under their own management for home supplies, or for the breeding of selected stock; very few as a matter of business, or for profit. The general system is, that the landowners make the permanent works on their estates, their income being paid in rent by tenant-occupiers; the tenants in their turn direct the cultivation, provide the farm-stock and implements and all the necessary capital and skill, and employ and pay the agricultural labourers by whose work the land is cultivated. The system is so general in the United Kingdom, that we really cannot be said to know any other, and yet, with reference to almost every country but our own, is so exceptional in Europe, that a more detailed description of it will be given in the next chapter. *[tenant-farmers.]*

The circumstances of Ireland eight years ago appeared favourable for the creation of a class of peasant proprietors, and Parliament resolved to give the principle a trial. Two opportunities presented themselves; first, in 1869, on the *[Peasant proprietors in Ireland.]*

disestablishment of the Church, which possessed upwards of 10,000 small holdings of land, in the benefices situated all over the country. The pre-emption of these was offered to the tenants on terms most favourable to them, both as to price and payment, and nearly two-thirds of the offers were promptly accepted. Again, in 1870, the Irish Land Act contained provisions expressly favouring the system; but, though great advantages in regard to terms of payment were also offered by that Act, the results hitherto have been comparatively small. The cause of the difference is very plain. In the first case the disposal of the lands was imperative, and did not occasion the subdivision of property; while the vendors, the Church Commissioners, having no one to consult but themselves, offered these small holdings at low fixed prices without competition. In the second case, on the other hand, it is the duty of the Landed Estates Court to get the best price they can for the landowner, who may very naturally object to allow small portions to be sold here and there out of his estate to suit the convenience of individual tenants. The farmers, moreover, begin to find themselves very secure in their possession as tenants, under the clauses of the Act, and have thus less inducement to buy the fee-simple; and the landowners, participating in the general prosperity, are no longer under pressure to sell at the low prices hitherto realised. It is thus not from any defects in the Land Act, but from the improved condition of the country, and the increased security given to farmers' capital by the Act itself, that this branch of it has become less operative than was anticipated.

CHAPTER V.

LANDOWNER, FARMER, AND LABOURER.

The landowners; their position, duties, and influence:

THE landowners are the capitalists to whom the land belongs. Their property comprises the soil and all that is beneath it, and the buildings and other permanent works upon it, required for the accommodation of the people, and of the working stock employed in its cultivation. Thus, where the land itself may be worth £35 an acre, the buildings, roads, fences, and drainage may have cost the landowners £15 an acre more. The landowner has thus two capitals in the land, one of which is permanent and growing rapidly in value with the prosperity of the country, the other liable to decay and occasioning cost in repair. In nearly all permanent improvements arising from the progress of agriculture he is also expected to share the cost. And he is necessarily concerned in the general prosperity and good management of his estate, and in the welfare of those who live upon it, with which his own is so closely involved. He takes a lead in the business of his parish, and from his class the magistrates who administer the criminal affairs of the county, and superintend its roads, its public buildings, and charitable institutions, are selected. Nor do his duties end here, for the landowner, from his position, is expected to be at the head of all objects of public utility, to subscribe to, and, if so inclined, to ride with the hounds, showing at once an example to the farmers and tradesmen, and meeting them on terms of neighbourly friendship and acquaintance. The same example is carried out in his intercourse with the clergy and schoolmaster, and his influence, where wisely exercised, is felt in the church, the school, the farm, and the cottage.

This class in the United Kingdom comprises a body of about 180,000, who possess among them the whole of the agricultural land from 10 acres upwards. The owners of less than 10 acres each hold not more than one-hundredth

their number, and the immense capital value of their property.

part of the land, and may here be regarded as householders only. The property of the landowners, independent of minerals, yields an annual rent of sixty-seven millions sterling, and is worth a capital value of two thousand millions. There is no other body of men in the country who administer so large a capital on their own account, or whose influence is so widely extended and universally present. From them the learned professions, the church, the army, and the public services are largely recruited.

The tenant-farmers; the proportionate extent of their holdings, and the emulation that exists among them.

The tenant-farmers are the second class, and a much more numerous one. Their business is the cultivation of the land, with a capital quite independent of that of the landowner. They occupy farms of very various extent, 70 per cent. of them under 50 acres each, 12 per cent. between 50 and 100 acres, and 18 per cent. farms of more than 100 acres each. 5,000 occupy farms of between 500 and 1,000 acres, and 600 occupy farms exceeding 1,000 acres. Many of them are men of liberal education, and some of these are found in most parishes and in every county. A spirit of emulation exists among them, elicited by county, provincial, and national exhibitions of agricultural stock, and by a natural desire, in a country where everything is open to comment, not to be behind their neighbours in the neatness, style, and success of their cultivation, or in the symmetry and condition of their live-stock. They are brought into the closest relations with their labourers, and although, occasionally, feelings of keen antagonism have arisen, there is generally a very friendly understanding between them. The farmer knows that it is for his interest that the labourers should find their position made so comfortable as to value it.

To the farmer is committed the management of the details of the parish, as those of the county to the landowner. His intimate knowledge of the condition of the labourer, and constant residence in the parish, fit him best for the duty of Overseer of the Poor, member of the Board of Guardians, Churchwarden, and Surveyor of the Roads. He is frank and hospitable to strangers, as a rule; in favour of the established political institutions of the country; loyal as a subject; generally available in case of need as a mounted yeoman; and constantly in requisition as a juryman in the Courts of Law.

Their numbers and capital. The farmers are six times as numerous as the landowners, there being 560,000 in Great Britain, and 600,000 in Ireland, the holdings there being on a smaller scale. They employ a vast capital in the aggregate, upwards of four hundred millions sterling, and, unlike that of the landowners, much of it is in daily use, circulating among tradesmen and labourers.

Land-agents. Between the landlords and farmers there is an intermediate class, the land-agents, to whom on most large estates the details of transacting business with the farmers, and looking after the cultivation and buildings and general condition of the property, are committed. These gentlemen, in most cases, are prepared by a course of special training and education for the very important and delicate duties thus entrusted to them. Where they possess such an amount of general knowledge as enables them to carry their employer with them in all equitable arrangements for maintaining the property in a state of high agricultural efficiency, they perform a most useful function, and add very greatly to the welfare and comfort of all connected with the estates which they administer. A very eminent living authority rests the tenure of property on the fulfilment of duty; and a most important part of that duty is to see that no good land upon it is suffered by neglect or mismanagement to remain unproductive.

The third class comprises the agricultural labourers, who are necessarily much more numerous than both landowners and tenants. They cannot be said to have any other capital than the furniture of their dwellings, their well-acquired experience in all the details of husbandry, and the bodily strength to use it. The English labourer, of the southern counties especially, has hitherto had but little education, except in his business. The Scotch have had their parish schools for three centuries, and the Irish a national school system for the last forty years. The legislation of 1876 has removed *The labourers:*

this blot on the English system, by enacting that no child shall be employed at any kind of labour until he is of the age of ten, nor above that age unless he can show a certain degree of proficiency in education. This excellent rule is a virtual compulsion of education, as parents and employers alike are liable to penalties for its infringement. And as it is now accompanied in all parts of the kingdom by the establishment of duly regulated schools, no child can avoid an elementary education.

<small>their state in some of the southern counties long a subject of reproach, but now mending.</small>

The state of the agricultural labourer of the southern counties has long been the subject of reproach, and, till a recent period, not without good reason. In many parishes the average rate of wages was below the means of maintaining a man's bodily strength adequate to good work, and the result was that two men at low wages were kept to do the work of one well-paid labourer. The employer was a loser by this; and though he might be aware of it, he could not help it, for there was a redundancy of labour seeking employment, and which had to be maintained either by wages or poor-rates.

The labourer himself was uneducated, having little knowledge of any district outside his own parish, no means of moving beyond it, while he risked the loss of his legal right to the parish relief in illness or old age if he left it. In such circumstances it was hardly possible for the agricultural labourer to attain any degree of independence. There was no margin for saving, no surplus out of which an enterprising man could make the venture of moving his labour to places in which it would command a better return. And during the long period that this continued, his condition was low, and still shows itself in his small stature and slow gait. From the pressure of this system he was at last emancipated by the extension of his legal right of relief from the parish to the Union, a district much more extensive, and by the simultaneous increase in the demand for labour arising from the rapid development of the other industrial resources of the country. The great extension of steam communication with America, and the encouragement thereby afforded to emigration, drew off rapidly the surplus agricultural population of Scotland and Ireland; wages in both countries quickly increased, and this soon extended its influence southwards. Agricultural labourers' unions were formed in the depressed districts just when this wholesome feeling was spreading throughout the country, and to their efforts much of the natural effect of other causes in producing a rise of wages has been ascribed. This increase of wages was attended by a most useful result, for it forced upon farmers the more extensive use of machinery, and, in the end, brought about a higher scale of wages to the labourer, while the additional cost to the farmer is met to some extent by superior skill, and greater economy in the application of labour. It is worthy of note that the increase of agricultural wages has been greatest in Scotland, where labourers' unions have not taken root.

Condition now better than at any previous period, comparing wages with the price of bread.

The general condition of the agricultural labourer was probably never better than it is at present. Compared with that of 300 years ago, in the time of Elizabeth, wages have risen sixfold, while the price of bread has only doubled. Two centuries later, in 1770, the farm-labourer's wages was 1s. 2d. a day, when the price of wheat was 46s. a quarter. In 1846, immediately before the repeal of the Corn Laws, wages were 1s. 7d., when wheat was 53s. At the present time wages have risen 60 per cent., while wheat has not increased in price. In other words, the labourer's earning power in procuring the staff of life, cost him five days' work to pay for a bushel of wheat in 1770, four days in 1840, and two and a half days in 1870. He is better lodged than he ever was before; though, in many parts of the country, there is still much room for improvement in that respect. Compared with the labourer in towns, his position is one of greater comfort; he lives in a better atmosphere, he is more free from anxiety, and has a closer and more friendly relation with his employers, and with the schoolmaster and clergyman of his parish. He is kind to animals, understands how to manage them, and in his family shows a good example, on the whole, of sobriety and industry.

F

Each of the three classes constantly recruited by changes of property and employment.

To these three classes are committed the agricultural interest and industry of the kingdom. The two first have duties entrusted to them by the constitution, for the management of the public and local interests of their counties and parishes, in addition to their special business as landowners and agriculturists. Each of the three classes is constantly being altered and recruited by changes and additions. Landed property of the value of several millions sterling a year changes hands, and as there is necessarily a larger body of persons capable of competing for small properties, there is a natural tendency to subdivision on sale. In every county many farms change their tenants at Lady Day or Michaelmas, new men with new ideas being substituted for the old, some of whom have died, some retired from business, and some moved elsewhere. Labourers move about more than they used to do, and learn something useful in each change, and large drafts of them pass off to the other industrial pursuits of the country, and to the colonies. The feeling of being bound to the soil or the parish of his birth has lost much of its strength, and every facility is now presented to the unmarried agricultural labourer for improving his position if he desires to alter it.

In short, our system is that of large capitalists owning the land; of smaller capitalists, each cultivating five times more of it than they would have means to do if they owned their farms; and of labourers free to carry their labour to any market which they consider most remunerative. It has been the gradual growth of experience in a country of moderate extent, where land is all occupied, where capital is abundant and constantly seeking investment in land; and where other industries than agriculture are always demanding recruits from the children of the agricultural labourer, who find, besides, a ready outlet in those British colonies where the soil and climate are not much different from that which they leave, and where their own language is spoken. And doubtless this facility of language has greatly helped the people of this country in encountering the trials and difficulties of emigration. But the want of it may be successfully overcome, as the example of Germany has proved in the tens of thousands of her people who have gone to the United States. There, and in the vast continent of Australia, there is room enough to take, with advantage, the surplus population of every country in Europe for many generations. Instead of struggling at home as labourers, or cultivators of small patches of land where nothing but the most sparing frugality enables them to live, the working men of all countries are invited and assisted by Australia to take a share on equal terms with our own people in the great enterprise of colonising a new continent, where liberty, order, and remunerative employment are offered to all comers; where the climate is pure and healthy for Europeans, and where every industry, agricultural, manufacturing, or mining, affords a field for enterprise.

The result of the system compared with that of other countries shows larger

A system is best tested by its fruits. Compared with all other countries, our threefold plan of landlord, farmer, and labourer, appears to yield larger returns, with fewer labourers, and from an equal extent of land. Our average produce of wheat is 28 bushels an acre, as against 16 in France, 16 in Germany, and 13 in Russia and the United States. We show a similar advantage in live-stock, both in quantity and quality. We have far more horses, cattle, and sheep in proportion to acreage than any other country, and in all these kinds there is a general superiority. Our most famous breeders of live-stock are the tenant-farmers. The best examples of farming are found in the same class. The improved breeds of cattle, the Leicester and Southdown sheep, and the extended use of machinery, manures, and artificial foods are chiefly due to them. And the neatness of the cultivation, the straight furrow, and the beautiful lines of drilled corn, the well-built ricks and docile horses, exhibit at once the strength and skill of the labourers. If that mode of husbandry which lessens the exchangeable value of bread and meat by an increase of production and supply is the best for the community, from whom a smaller proportion of their labour is required for the purchase of their food, then our system of subdivision of labour

returns at less cost.

by landowner, farmer, and labourer, the three interests engaged in its production, will stand a favourable comparison with that of any other country.

Special features presented by it in each of the three countries; in England,

There are characteristic features in the business relation between the landowner and farmer which deserve notice, in its application to the three countries, England, Scotland, and Ireland. In England the general system is tenancy at will, by which the connection may be terminated on six months' notice. The result is, that the notice is rarely given, changes of tenancy are comparatively few, and systems of management are slowly altered.

in Scotland,

In Scotland there has long been tenancy on a nineteen years' lease. The certainty of the tenure up to a fixed time prompts immediate enterprise to make the most of that definite period, and changes of tenant at its conclusion have become frequent. There can be no doubt that this has been attended with a more hearty and ready appreciation of improved processes on the part of both landlord and tenant, and a higher scale of wages to the labourer. It still needs, however, some equitable rules to secure continuance of the tenant's interest in good farming to the close of the lease. And the Scotch tenants are also hampered by an unreasonable law which prohibits them from transferring their leases even to a solvent and unobjectionable successor, and, still worse, from bequeathing the lease to their widows or any of their children except the heir-at-law. Ireland has a system of its own. <small>in Ireland</small> Till a very recent period the tenant made nearly all improvements, such as they were. He reclaimed the waste, built his own poor habitation, and he and his family occupied the land, and subdivided it amongst them. He thus tacitly acquired a hold on the soil much greater than in the sister countries, and which was generally acquiesced in by the landlords, many of whom were non-residents. These three systems were the natural growth of circumstances, and have become deeply intertwined with the habits and feelings of the agricultural classes in the several countries.

Three-fourths of the land in England have long been held by a comparatively small body <small>Origin of tenancy-at-will in England.</small>

of great landowners. From the Revolution in 1688 till the Reform Bill of 1831, all political power was in their hands. They were the patrons of agriculture, and their tenants, being accustomed to continue undisturbed, neither asked nor expected legal security of tenure. But habit and custom gave such security in reality, though not in law; and to this day there are families of tenants-at-will who can count back a longer period of unbroken succession in their farms than the great landowner at whose will they hold them. The first Reform Bill gave tenant-farmers, paying a rent of £50 and upwards, the right to vote in the election of members of Parliament, and thus strengthened their hold on the consideration of their landlord, but at the same time gave him an unfortunate interest in the continuance of a system which kept them dependent on his will. This continued for one generation more, until in 1867 the franchise was lowered to £12, and in 1871 vote by ballot introduced. By those measures the numbers and political strength of the tenant-farmer class were largely increased. Household suffrage in counties is believed to be not far off, and thus the hitherto paramount political influence of the landowner in the counties is gradually being replaced by the wider basis of the representation of each of their varied interests. The first result of the latest extension of the constituency, and their protection by ballot, has been a strong agitation on the part of the farmers to obtain a legal right to be compensated, on removal, for their unexhausted manures and improvements. Simultaneously with it, a labourers' league has been formed in some districts to concentrate the latent power of the dispersed but numerous body of agricultural labourers. Both of these movements have been attended with a moderate measure of success. The Agricultural Holdings Act, passed two years ago, recognises for the first time a legal right in the English farmer to compensation for unexhausted improvements, cumbered indeed with conditions which have made it unsatisfactory to both parties. A considerable step has, however, been gained, as all parties are brought to look carefully into their position, and thus the mutual connection, while losing something of sentiment, will in time gain more of business and enterprise.

<small>Landowner's necessities prompted leases in Scotland.</small>

In Scotland the necessities of the landowners prompted them, at a much earlier period, to seek relief from the embarrassments of entail by obtaining legislative power to borrow money for the improvement of their settled property. And, when the means were thus provided for executing permanent works, the energies of the tenant-farmers were wisely enlisted in carrying these into remunerative effect by the now well-recognised form of a lease of nineteen years, at a fixed rent, to assure the tenants such a period of possession as should at once evoke their best exertions. This system has now been in practice for three generations, and its results are seen in a higher state of general cultivation than that of the sister countries; greater competition for farms, and a higher scale of rent; more independence; and at least as keen an intelligence shown in adopting improvements. For a long period the Scotch landowners have been compelled to look into the management of their property in a different manner from those of England. Upon them the liability was directly placed of finding the money for the public establishments of their counties, the churches, prisons, and police. They had the determination of questions of road-making; and having to contribute directly a large proportion of the county expenditure, they took an active interest in its administration. This brought them into closer business contact with the farmers; and recent legislation has tended to increase this connection by the principle of imposing all county rates in certain proportion directly on landowners and farmers, and giving to both a representation at the same county or parish board. There is thus a better fusion of the two interests than in England, and a readier appreciation on the part of the landowner of the outlays requisite on his part to enable his tenant to make the most of the land he farms. The time seems rapidly approaching when the Scotch system of equal valuation and rating, imposed directly upon both landowner and farmer, will be imitated in England, and lead to the principle of local administration in each county by representatives of every interest at a county board.

<small>Non-residence of land-owners produced system of middle-men in Ireland, and its consequent evils.</small>

In Ireland the relation between landlord and tenant is altogether different from that of England and Scotland. Previous to the famine of 1846, the great landowners were non-resident, and the land was still in a great measure in the hands of middle-men on leases for lives, with leave to subdivide and sublet for the same time. These men had no permanent interest in the property; their business was to make an income out of it at the least cost, and their intermediate position severed the otherwise natural connection between landlord and tenant. The famine of 1846 prostrated the class of middle-men entirely, and brought the landowner and the real tenants face to face. But the hold which the latter had been permitted to obtain led them to consider the landowner very much as only the holder of the first charge on the land; and they were in the habit of selling and buying their farms among themselves subject to this charge, a course which, as a matter of practice, was tacitly accepted by the landowner. He had security for his rent in the money paid by an incoming tenant, who, for his own safety, required the landowner's consent to the change of tenancy, and the landowner's agent then received the "price" of the farm (for that was the term used), and handed it over to the outgoing tenant, after deducting all arrears of rent. This suited the convenience of landowners, the most of whom had no money to spend on improvements, many of them non-resident and taking little interest in the country, and dealing with a numerous body of small tenants with whom they seldom came into personal contact. In the north of Ireland this custom of sale became legally recognised as tenant-right. The want of it in other parts of Ireland produced an agitation which ultimately led to the Irish Land Act, under which legislative protection is given to customs capable of proof. The custom of "selling" the farm, subject to the approval of the landowner, by a tenant on yearly tenure, is rapidly gaining ground in Ireland; and so firmly are the people imbued with this idea of their rights, that the clauses of the Irish Land Act, which enable the tenant, by the aid of a loan of Government money, on very easy terms, to purchase the proper ownership of his farm, are rarely acted upon, from the belief that the farm is already his, under the burden of a moderate rent-charge to his nominal landlord. Circumstances have thus brought about a situation in which the landowner cannot deal with the same freedom with his property as in England or Scotland, either in the selection of his tenants or in the fair readjustment of rent, and this has, in a great measure, arisen naturally from the neglect by the landlord of his proper duties, in not himself executing those indispensable permanent improvements, which the tenant was thus obliged to undertake, and who in this way established for himself a claim to a co-partnership in the soil itself.

CHAPTER VI.

LAND IMPROVEMENT.

HAVING now endeavoured to explain the respective positions of the three interests engaged in the cultivation of the soil in each of the three countries forming the United Kingdom, I proceed to consider the circumstances which embarrass the free action of a large proportion of the landowners, and the modes by which these have been more or less overcome. A very large proportion of the land is held by tenants for life under strict settlement, a condition which prevents the power of sale, and it is also frequently burdened with payments to other members of the family, and in many cases with debt. The nominal income is thus often very much reduced, and the apparent owner of five thousand a year may have little more than half of it to spend. In such cases there is no capital available for the

Settlements and incumbrances hinder the free action of many landowners in the management of their property.

improvements which a landowner is called upon to make, in order to keep his property abreast of the advance in agricultural practice. This was pressingly felt at the time of the repeal of the Corn Laws, and the withdrawal of protective duties from native produce. Parliament, therefore, when it enacted a free import of the necessaries of life, provided State loans on favourable terms to the landowners for the drainage and reclamation of their estates.

Expedients adopted to overcome this.

The potato disease of 1846 and 1847 was a serious calamity at the time, but it was the occasion from which arose the great stride made in agricultural enterprise in this country during the last thirty years. It led at once to the removal of all protective duties on foreign agricultural produce, and obtained for the people of this country access to supplies from foreign lands, where wages were lower and good land more abundant. Landowners and farmers bestirred themselves to meet the inevitable competition to which they became exposed; and their efforts were promptly aided by the State with reproductive loans to tide them over the early years of trial. As the sums voted by Parliament for these loans became exhausted, Land Improvement Companies were formed to carry on the good work on the principles which had already proved successful, the companies necessarily charging somewhat higher terms than those which the credit of the State had enabled it to afford without loss.

The State loans were limited in Great Britain to drainage and reclamation, the landowners being left to their own resources for buildings, roads, and fences. In Ireland these were and still are included, that country having always been favoured in matters of State assistance. The rate of payment was by annual instalments of 6½ per cent., which in twenty-two years redeemed the principal, and at the same time paid the annual interest at 3½ per cent. In many cases the tenant undertook the whole of this annual payment in addition to his rent, and the landowner thus had his land permanently improved, and returned to him free of all charge at the end of twenty-two years. Not unfrequently the landowner was satisfied with 5 per

State loans for drainage and reclamation of land, and in Ireland for buildings also, issued on favourable terms:

cent. from his tenant, and paid 1½ out of his own pocket for this permanent advantage. Especially was this the case in regard to buildings, the return from which is not so direct or immediate as from drainage or reclamation.

<small>followed by loans from Companies.</small>

The same principle is followed by the Land Improvement Companies, whose loans, like those of the State, are secured by priority over all other charges, but continue for twenty-five or thirty years, according to the rate annually paid. It has been proposed to extend the term still farther, in order to reduce the rate of annual repayment; but this is a questionable advantage, for each generation has improvements of its own to carry out, and it is a good general rule that the cost of the past should be paid off before new charges are placed on the land.

<small>Total amount so expended.</small>

The total amount of money charged on the land of the United Kingdom for agricultural improvements under the system of periodical redemption, in the last thirty years, amounts to about fifteen millions sterling—twelve in Great Britain and three in Ireland. About eight millions of it was advanced by the State, and seven millions by private companies. A large proportion of the first has now been repaid, having been returned to the public exchequer, principal and interest, and is no longer a charge upon the land. Two-thirds of the whole have been spent on drainage, the remainder on farm-buildings, labourers' cottages, embanking, water-courses, farm roads, reclamation, planting for shelter, and enclosing. The expenditure through such loans goes on with great regularity at an average of half a million sterling a year, and the loans are being redeemed and the charge extinguished at about the same rate. The extent of work still to be done far exceeds what has been accomplished, and so many new demands arise to meet the changes in husbandry that the system is likely to be a permanent one. It may therefore be useful to consider its present mode of working, the objections which have been made to it, and whether any improvement can be introduced which might facilitate its operation.

An inquiry into this subject was undertaken by the House of Lords in 1873. The Com-

Inquiry by Parliament into

the mode of working these loans, and their results.

mittee comprised men of acknowledged eminence on both sides of politics, great landowners conversant with such subjects, and having more or less practical knowledge of agricultural affairs. Twenty-three witnesses were examined from various parts of the kingdom, all of whom had experience of the system. Various instances were adduced to show the unremunerative nature of certain improvements, the explanation of which was either injudicious and imperfect execution of the works, or inadequacy of capital, or energy, or knowledge, to follow them up by good culture; want of knowledge and experience on the part of the landowner or his agent, or the usual circumstances of a similar nature which are found here and there to occur in all large operations, which must often be unwittingly entrusted to weak or dishonest management. As this inquiry embraced the execution of works in all parts of Great Britain, spread over a period of twenty-six years, and embracing an expenditure then exceeding ten millions sterling, the comparatively few and exceptional instances of failure might be taken as a strong proof of the general success of the system. Except in such buildings as required restoration from the continued neglect of landowners to repair—a case very common both north and south—some return seems always to be reckoned upon, even for expenditure on new buildings. On all other kinds of improvement there was a general testimony to their remunerative character. And those of the witnesses most competent to speak, the tenant-farmers, who had themselves repaid the cost of the works, declared that they had received from the money spent on land-improvement much more than a return of capital and interest. *General testimony to their remunerative character.*

The Committee very truly remark that it is an anomaly that private transactions should be submitted to the control of a Government office. This was perfectly legitimate, so long as the money advanced was a public loan. When the supply of public money ceased, and that of private persons or companies was substituted, the existing Government machinery of inspection and control, which had been found on the whole to work well, was continued by Parlia- *Object of continuing Government control after issue of public money ceased.*

ment on the ground that the improvement of the land of this country was a matter of public interest. But this was not with the view of protecting the interests of the remainder-man and mortgagee, for that is no part of the duty of Government; but in order to give a first charge on the inheritance, and so enable landowners, whether under settlement or otherwise, to obtain money for improving their estates, (which is an object of public importance,) at a lower rate of interest than would otherwise have been possible. This preferential charge could be given only with the tacit assent of other parties already creditors of the estate; and the condition which hitherto has assured that assent has been the certificate, under statutory powers, of an acknowledged Government authority, that their security had not been thereby injuriously affected. The continuance of the Government inspection has thus been wholly in the interest of the landowner, especially if he is under settlement or entail, in which condition the tenant for life is otherwise unable to raise money for the improvement of his property.

Besides the public and private loans spent on land improvement, a much larger sum has been laid out on the same object by landowners from their own resources.

It may be useful to consider in their order the several objects of land-improvement, and the return they are capable of yielding under suitable economical management.

<small>Land drainage one of the most certainly remunerative improvements.</small>

The first improvement, in all cases where it is required, is drainage, for until the land is freed from stagnant water, and thus rendered capable of yielding its fullest assistance to the further efforts of the agriculturist, all other outlay is vain. There is never any difficulty in deciding upon the expediency of drainage in these islands, because wherever it is required, and is judiciously executed, it at once becomes remunerative. The under drainage of arable and good grass-land, in a climate where drainage is advantageous, renders the land so much warmer and more wholesome for plants and animals, everything upon it becomes so much more thrifty, and all operations so much more easy and certain in their results, that it is sure to pay. No doubt the increasing cost of labour and materials is seriously felt, but the value of land and of most kinds of agricultural produce is likewise increasing.

Greater caution required in expenditure on farm buildings.

With regard to outlay on farm buildings, there is not the same certainty of return. Farm buildings are of two kinds, those for the accommodation of live-stock and the manipulation of the crop, and those for the housing of the farmer and farm labourers. In regard to the first, it is only necessary to refer to the increasing prices of live-stock to show the advantage of making adequate and comfortable provision for their food and shelter. But the time has gone by for great corn barns. The corn is now much more economically treated by stacking it in the field where it grows, and threshing it out by locomotive engine-power when required. The partial conversion of these large barns into feeding-sheds, or in the grazing counties into hay-sheds, is the best mode of turning them to account; and where farm-buildings have been kept by the proprietor in good repair, their conversion to objects of modern husbandry need not be very costly. It is only where they have been completely neglected, and require entire renewal, that the expense is greater than can be met by the immediate return. Even then it is capable of proof that the economy of labour and of food, the better quality of the manure, and the greater thrift of the stock, will, as a rule, be ample compensation for the charge. Additions to existing buildings for a specific object, planned and executed with judgment, will always be remunerative. But the more common fault of putting up very costly buildings, planned with little reference to the value and extent of the farm, or little practical knowledge on the part of land-agent or architect, too surely ends in disappointment to both landowner and farmer.

Labourers' cottages are reckoned the least remunerative of all. New cottages, even though built in blocks of two or four together, cannot at present be built by contract for less than £150 each, if planned with due regard to comfort and decency, and at a greater cost if the *Labourers' dwellings, when judiciously placed, as remunerative as any other outlay of landowners' capital.*

expense of haulage of materials is included. To repay this in twenty-five years, both principal and interest, a weekly rent of 4s. is required. But labourers in the southern counties have been unable to pay more than 1s. or 2s. out of their weekly wages, so that the landowner who lets good cottages at that rent is really paying also 2s. or 3s. a week towards the wages of his farmer's labourers. By this, all the parties are misled. The landowner's duty to his estate is to provide it with all permanent buildings required for its proper cultivation. He must do so if he cultivates the land himself, and he ought equally to do so if he lets it to be cultivated by another. The farmer, whether landowner or tenant, must then furnish the farm with the "plant," the live and dead stock necessary for its cultivation. Both parties are entitled to look for a return for their investment; the landowner's safe and improving capital yielding him a smaller annual return than the farmer's, which is liable to the vicissitudes of seasons, and wear and tear, and must also cover his personal industry and skill. The labourers' dwellings are as indispensable as the stables and barns, and no arable farm can be said to be complete which has not the command of an adequate number of cottages for the workpeople. These, with the farm and all other necessary buildings, should be let to the farmer at a rent which should include a fair return on the landlord's capital, and the farmer and the labourer should be left to deal with each other on the basis of adequate remuneration for useful service, regulated by the ultimate rule of demand and supply. On this footing the return on labourers' cottages will become as remunerative as that of any other outlay of landowners' capital, because it will be controlled by the real necessity and requirements of the farm.

This will apply chiefly in cases where new cottages are attached to farms, and fresh outlay for that object is to be made. But, in the vast majority of cases, labourers' cottages already exist in sufficient numbers. Better cottages are required in many parts of the country, rather than more of them. It has been well ascertained that during the last thirty years the

Better cottages wanted rather than more of them.

agricultural population has diminished. The circumstances which have led to that continue in full strength. Increased facilities of locomotion between different parts of the country, and for emigration across the seas, tend more and more to carry off the energetic portion of the agricultural population. This has raised the rate of farm wages and the cost of cultivating arable land. The prosperity of the wage-earning class in other occupations has, at the same time, vastly increased the demand for butcher's meat and dairy produce, and so greatly increased the returns from grass land. The natural result is a gradual conversion of suitable arable land to grass, and this diminution of extent is accompanied also by the introduction of labour-saving machines. There is thus in both ways a tendency to a diminution of our agricultural population, the one operating in carrying off the ablest to more remunerative fields of industry, the other in lessening the home demand for agricultural labour. It is a fact of great importance in the consideration of this question that, within the period between the census of

1861 and 1871, there has been a decrease of the country population in every county of England except five, and it is only in the suburban counties and in the manufacturing and mining districts that an increase has taken place. Future provision for agricultural labourers' dwellings ought therefore to be in the direction of improvement rather than increase.

Abundant proof might easily be adduced from most parts of the country that on the main heads of agricultural improvement there should be no lack of good return. The fact that the outlay goes on without diminution, notwithstanding the great increase in the cost of labour and materials, would alone upset all reasoning, and isolated instances, to the contrary. A very instructive paper on this part of the subject was produced by the managing director of the Lands Improvement Company. It showed a return of forty cases of outlays, not picked cases, but taken as they happened to come, with the increased rentals subsequent to the improvements. Upon an outlay in the aggregate of £195,000 there was an increased rental of £31,000. This

Examples of remunerative expenditure.

increase had been obtained within seven to ten years. In only five instances did the increase fall short of repaying the annual charge which redeems the principal as well as the interest. In every other case it left a profit beyond this, in many cases a large profit. On the whole, the increase is equal to a return of 15 per cent. on the expenditure, and if this is capitalised at the common estimate of thirty years' purchase of land rent, the sum expended will be found to have been increased more than fourfold. If landowners generally could reckon on anything like the average return of these forty cases, they would have the means, under the Lands Improvement Acts, of improving their estates, not only without present loss, but with a large immediate profit.

But no distinction was made or could be made in this return between that increment which arose from improvements and the general increase of rent due to the prosperity of the country, the increased value of produce, and the development of particular districts by the opening of railways and roads. Still in one way or other the landowner in these cases has been made entirely safe.

And in the nature of things in this country such must be the case wherever reasonable judgment has been shown in expenditure on land improvement. The improver is dealing with a limited article, for the produce of which there is an ever-increasing demand. Nature has given us a climate more favourable to the production of meat and milk, vegetables and grass, than that of any other European State. These, in proportion to their value, are the least costly in labour, and therefore the least affected by a rise of wages. The growing demand for them, and their consequently increasing value, exercise a constant pressure for increased production, which can still to some extent be obtained by improving the land we have. A large proportion of the improvable land under cultivation admits of this, and much of that vast tract which has hitherto been left to nature might also be profitably reclaimed for the rearing of sheep and cattle.

CHAPTER VII.

RECENT RISE IN THE VALUE OF LAND.

Great rise in the value of land since the repeal of the Corn Laws, only partly due to the outlay of capital in improvements.

THERE has been, within the last twenty years, a very considerable increase in the value of land in this country. The income-tax returns are most instructive on this point, and, as they show the rental of land in England, Scotland, and Ireland separately, they afford the means of comparing the rate of improvement in each country. That improvement does not seem to have begun in England till 1858, the gross annual value of "Lands" in 1857 having been returned at £50,000 less in that year than in 1846. From 1858 the rise has been progressive and continuous, and with an average increase of £470,000 a year. The rise seems to have begun somewhat earlier in Scotland, and the average yearly increase has been £82,000. The returns from Ireland cannot be distinguished prior to

1862, and show an average yearly increase, from that year, of £39,000. The total rise within a period of eighteen years has been a little over 20 per cent.; but, as will be seen by the annexed Table, the proportion of increase on the Scotch rental has been greater than on that of England. The small rise in Ireland presents a striking contrast to England and Scotland. The capital value of the total increase at the present selling price of land in this country will be reckoned something prodigious, especially by those of us who are old enough to recall the dismal prophecies of the agricultural ruin which would surely follow the free admission of foreign corn.

Gross Annual Value of Land Assessed to the Income-Tax in 1857 and 1875.

	1857.	1875.	Increase.	Increase per cent.	Capital Value of Increase at 30 Years' Purchase.
	£	£	£		£
England...	41,177,000	50,125,000	8,948,000	21	268,440,000
Scotland...	5,932,000	7,493,000	1,561,000	26	46,830,000
Ireland, from 1862	8,747,000	9,293,000	546,000	6	16,380,000
	55,856,000	66,911,000	11,055,000	...	331,650,000

This vast increase in the value of landed property within the short period of twenty years is very remarkable. It has been already shown that the improvement expenditure effected by loans has been fifteen millions. If we assume that even three times as much has been effected during the same period by private capital without loans, we here see that the capital wealth of the owners of landed property has been increased by three hundred and thirty-one millions sterling in these twenty years, at a cost to them which probably has not exceeded sixty millions. This increase, as elsewhere explained, has arisen chiefly from the great advance in the consumption and value of meat and dairy produce, and is thus only in part the result of land improvement.

Greatest rise has been in the grazing counties, and in Scotland: the cause of this.

But though in the aggregate the landowners of England have become richer by more than one-fifth, and those of Scotland by more than one-fourth, the progress has not been uniform. In the purely corn districts, and on the chalk and sands of the drier counties, where grass does not thrive, the increase has been small. On the poor clays there has been none. It has been greatest in the grazing counties and in the west and north. The increase shown in Scotland deserves special attention. In that country the larger proportion of grazing-land no doubt partly explains this; but, on the other hand, entails are more strict, and land is understood to be more heavily mortgaged than in England, so that in these respects Scotland has no advantage. It was this greater disability of the entailed Scotch proprietor which drove him earlier to seek a remedy. A little more than a century ago, in 1770, the first Improvement of Land Act was passed, the famous Montgomery Act, the preamble of which clearly explains its origin. "Whereas much mischief arises to the public, which must daily increase so long as the law allowing such entails subsists, if some remedy be not provided," and then it provided a remedy very similar in principle to the Drainage Acts passed for both countries eighty years later. But the power of raising money would not alone have sufficed. It was necessary also to take care that that money should be wisely expended, and the astute heads which devised the Montgomery Act enlisted the aid of the tenant-farmers, by giving them the security of nineteen years' leases, and thus obtaining their co-operation in the execution of the works, and in the subsequent operations necessary to make them remunerative. This co-operation between landlord and tenant in Scotland had been in full action for more than two generations before the Drainage Loans introduced by Sir Robert Peel in 1848, when both landlord and tenant in Scotland at once eagerly availed themselves of the very liberal terms on which these were offered; and that goes on to this day. The facilities given by the Improvement of Land Act, 1864, which enables limited landowners to operate with their own means without the intervention of the Improvement Companies, were at once recognised in Scotland, which has availed itself of them to an extent six times greater, in proportion, than England. In Scotland, as was stated by one of the witnesses, " the tenants are practically the applicants for improvement loans." They readily meet their landlords much more than half way in contributing to the repayment; and instead of lagging behind, or waiting to be spurred on to further enterprise, they compete even too much with each other for the possession of farms on terms which have now become more remunerative to the landowners than to themselves. There is not in England, generally, a similar spirit of agricultural enterprise.

To what is this difference between the two countries to be attributed? Chiefly to three causes, in which the Scotch landowner has the advantage: earlier education in, and appreciation of, the benefits of land improvement; a better knowledge of the business of landowning; and the general system of leases. To the first, reference has already been made. The better knowledge of their business has naturally flowed from it to the Scotch landowners. They are trained to it by fathers who have been in their day likewise taught to look into the management of their property. Sir Walter Scott mentions the discussions with which his youth was familiar when visiting his country relations,

The Scotch landowner better trained to his business.

the comparative merits of "long" and "short" sheep, the reclamation of waste, and the advantage in a bare country of sheltering woods. "Aye be sticking in a tree," was the dying advice of an old Scotch laird to his son, "it will be growing when you're sleeping." The "home" farm was always found in the personal occupation of the Scotch landowner, and the Edinburgh University has for many years had a Chair of Agriculture. It is true that among the greater landowners of Scotland the English schools and universities have long had a special attraction, but even their tone has failed to eradicate from the young Scotchman's mind the inborn love of the farms and fields, and the country employments of his fathers.

Landowning the only business in which special training is not deemed necessary.

This knowledge of business is a matter of great moment to those who employ so vast a capital as the English landowners, a capital far beyond the entire value of our railways, mines, ironworks, canals, and gasworks put together. Men of the highest capacity, with special training and qualifications, are employed in the management of these. Constant watchfulness of the progress of invention, by which large results may be obtained on a given expenditure, is absolutely necessary to procure a profit in the general competition. The landowners of large estates entrust the management of their property to agents, more or less qualified, many very capable, but often hampered by the pressing need of their employer for the largest return of rental at the least cost. The landowner himself too seldom takes such an active and intelligent interest in the details of management as would convince him of the need to keep his farms in a similar state of high working order. It is not with him really a question of business. Let us take, by way of comparison, a manufacturer, merchant, or shipowner, employing each a capital equal to that of a landowner who has a rental of £5,000 a year. What would be thought of the prospects of a woollen manufacturer who, without the slightest preparation or special knowledge, embarked £100,000 in that business? Or of a man who took over a mercantile concern of the same extent, without having ever before written or read a business letter? Or of a young military officer giving up his commission to take the direction and responsibility of a great shipowning house? And yet this is in effect what is done every day by the majority of English landowners. They complain that the business so undertaken "is not sufficiently lucrative to offer much attraction to capital." And people are surprised that within the narrow limits of the British Isles, with a teeming, wealthy, meat-consuming people, so large a proportion of the cultivated land is still permitted to remain only partially productive.

<small>Security for tenant's capital, whether by leases or otherwise, should be given.</small>

The third point of difference between the two countries is the system of yearly tenancy in England, while leases of nineteen and twenty-one years may be said to be the rule in Scotland and the exception in England. It is in the nature of a yearly tenancy that there should be insecurity. Agricultural investments demand time to be fully remunerative. How can a man subject at any time to a year's notice to quit be expected to improve? That he does so in very many cases is due to the confidence of a long-standing connection between landlord and tenant. There does not live a more upright honourable man in any class than the average English landowner. But, with every acknowledgment of his desire to be just and fair in his dealings with his tenantry, it is vain to look for enterprise and progress where there is no real security. Whether that may be best attained under the Agricultural Holdings Act, or by special agreement without a lease, or by giving such security with two years' notice in addition to a lease, in one way or other security must be given to induce such an adequate flow of capital into the business of farming as will render it effective.

Owners in fee-simple, as well as tenants for life, very frequently use the powers given by the Land Improvement Acts. The principle of annual repayment of the loan, by which the estate is at once put under improvement and the debt redeemed, commends itself to every man who desires to retain and improve his property. He borrows, at a fixed rate of interest, on a security the augmenting value of which is all his own. Besides this, there are few landowners who have not either inherited, or found it necessary themselves to create, mortgages on their estates. This is common to all countries, and no change in the laws affecting land is likely to alter it. The limited owner and the full owner are alike subject to it. If further expenditure is required, the money in the ordinary way must be raised on less advantageous terms than the previous loans. It probably cannot be raised on any terms by the limited owner. But the admirable principle of Sir Robert Peel's Drainage Loans, the essence of which is that no charge shall be sanctioned which does not promise a return greater than the annual cost of a gradual repayment of the debt, may, without injustice to the previous creditor, permit them to be made a prior charge upon the land, and will thus secure the most advantageous terms to the borrower, whether he holds under settlement or in fee-simple.

Admirable principle of Drainage Loans.

But there are many cases of land improvement which can be only partially reached by these Acts, and which require to be dealt with in a different manner. In the home counties,

Extended powers of sale in the case of settled estates would be

for instance, and in the neighbourhood of some very advantageous. of our great centres of population, there are large tracts of comparatively infertile land, let at low rents as farms, and yielding little satisfactory return to anybody connected with them. Cases may be met with where the limited owner, who has inherited such a property from a succession of men in a similar position of legal incapacity, finds himself, in the midst of general progress, constrained to keep perhaps half a dozen parishes in a state almost of stagnation. The country itself is most likely well-timbered and very picturesque, with easy railway access to the metropolis or town, and highly suitable for residential occupation. He could sell it readily, if he had the power, in small properties for that purpose, retaining still an important family estate. It would not be difficult to point out cases in which this might be done with immense advantage to the landowner, the neighbourhood, and the public. Take, for example, a limited owner of 10,000 acres of such land, yielding a gross rent of £10,000. If he were enabled to sell 2,000 acres, which might fetch a residential price of £100 an acre, or £200,000, retaining his family seat and 8,000 acres: his rental would then be £8,000, plus the interest at 4 per cent. of £200,000 = £8,000. These sums together would make an income of £16,000, or 60 per cent. more than he had before. He would thus at once find himself in funds and in spirits to go on with the improvement of the remainder of his estate, while the neighbourhood would have the advantage of a circulation of fresh capital and ideas, to brighten a scene formerly rendered gloomy by dissatisfied indifference. Landowners who are precluded by entail or settlement from using this natural advantage of their position, are deprived of an incalculable benefit to themselves and their families.

<small>Settlements should be limited to lives in being.</small>

To a certain extent this has already been discovered, and there are probably no settlements of land now made without considerable powers of sale. The principle is recognised, and may with great benefit be extended and made general. Settlements of land to a limited extent, like settlements of any other kind of property, are likely to continue. I desire to avoid any discussion at present of their advantage, or otherwise, as a question of polity, but am anxious to see them, at least, limited to lives in being, with large powers of sale, so as not to hamper in the smallest degree the most beneficial disposition of the land. This, with an improved system of land transfer, long promised and anxiously hoped for by men of all parties, will render the country less dependent on palliative measures, such as the Land Improvement Acts. But these have proved, and continue to be found, of indispensable service, as, without them, the improvement of land would still be impossible over a large portion of this kingdom.

But even increased freedom for the energies of the landowner will fail if not adequately backed by an intelligent and enterprising tenantry. The rapid changes which have taken place in late years, both in the improvement of live-stock and in the better cultivation of the land, are in the main due to them. The vast business which has grown up in the importation *The large capital of tenant-farmers entitled to legal security.*

and manufacture of manures and feeding-stuffs shows their willingness to enter upon new lines of expenditure which promise useful results. They have a large capital at stake, and they justly desire freedom of action in regard to cultivation, and security for that portion of their capital which, being necessarily incorporated with the soil to produce a future return, may be confiscated wherever it remains unprotected by contract or by law.

CHAPTER VIII.

THE GOVERNMENT IN ITS CONNECTION WITH AGRICULTURE.

THERE is no Minister of Agriculture in Great Britain, and no attempt is made by Government to interfere with the cultivation of the soil, or between the landowners, the tenants, and the labourers. There are no State flocks, or herds, or horse-breeding establishments, nor any State schools of agriculture. In Ireland such schools, and several experimental farms, were established at the cost of the Government, at the time of the potato famine. In the disorganised state in which that country then was, some benefit ensued. But the general principle of our political system is that every trade and business should be self-supporting, subordinate only to the general laws, and controlled by the rule of free competition. The political influence possessed by the landed interests insures for

No Minister of Agriculture, and no Government control exercised, or State schools, or State flocks or herds maintained by Government.

them adequate representation in the Government, and their great wealth endows them with the means of promoting all objects of general interest to them as a class. The Royal Agricultural Societies in England and Ireland, and the Highland and Agricultural Society of Scotland, are the self-supporting national institutions of each kingdom for the promotion of agriculture. And, besides great provincial societies in various parts of the country, there are in every county one or more local Agricultural Societies for the same object. These are all self-supporting, having neither stipend from the State, nor being subject to its control. The good result of this principle is seen in the successful manner in which they have evoked friendly competition amongst all classes connected with the land, and disseminated in every part of the country a knowledge of the best breeds of live-stock, and of the most improved instruments and processes of agricultural development.

The Inclosure Commission the The only department of the State which has a direct connection with the land is the

Inclosure Office, which combines several objects, more or less appertaining to landed property, but with no power to interfere except when applied to for the means of facilitating improvements. The costs of all proceedings effected through this department are provided by those who make use of it. Its original object was to promote the inclosure of waste lands, and thereby to increase the home produce of food, and afford increased employment to the agricultural labourers. These objects, so far as they were necessary, have to a great extent been otherwise accomplished, and the agricultural labourer has become happily independent of such aid. The duty of this branch of the office now is not to promote inclosure with the object of dividing the land amongst severalty owners, except in cases where by no other means could its improvement be effected, but to encourage the improvement of "commons" under a system of regulation, by which the land may be drained, planted for ornament and shelter, and the surface be improved for pasturage, without excluding the public from its

only State department directly connected with the land.

enjoyment by subdivision into severalty owner-ship. Advantage of the office has from time to time been taken by Parliament for objects of an analogous character. The Drainage and Land Improvement Acts are administered by this Commission, the object of these Acts being, as already explained, to permit landowners to borrow money for permanent improvements, and to charge their lands with the cost of these on the principle of such annual payments as within a definite period will reimburse both principal and interest. The control exercised by the Government department insures that the proposed improvement shall be both beneficial and well executed, and that the future possessor of the property may not find himself on his succession called on to pay for unprofitable outlays made by his predecessor. But any Government control in such circumstances is really the fruit of the artificial system of entail and settlement.

Its various functions.

The office is also entrusted with the formation of commissions for the drainage of districts liable to floods, under which works embracing

Formation of Main Drainage Commissions.

large areas of country are carried out under a general system, the cost being levied on the landowners in proportion to the advantage they receive. In the execution of this duty it has been found that the applicants in many cases have erred in not including the whole of the area which should naturally fall under one control, and so failing to secure uniformity over the whole of the catchment basin affected.

Floods in river valleys in autumn, and winter, and spring, provide rich irrigation for the land, the mud in which subsides when the waters are for a time partially stagnant. They are very beneficial if not permitted to remain too long. Land subject to such floods should never be broken up from grass, as in no other way can it in this country be more profitably used. Before under-drainage became so general, the floods came down much more loaded with sediment, and therefore much more enriching than now, when the rains of the uplands pass through and are filtered by the soil. Summer floods are injurious, but they are rare, and if once in twenty years they injure or even carry

Floods beneficial, except where permitted to remain too long stagnant.

off the hay, there is some compensation in the heavy crops of aftermath that follow. If the natural beds of the rivers were kept free from obstruction there would be far more benefit than injury from floods.

But in earlier times, before steam-power was known, water-power was found a valuable aid for both mills and navigation. Weirs and dams were then constructed, and water-rights have grown up which greatly hamper arterial drainage. Towns on the river-banks, though generally built above flood-mark, are injured by long-continued floods; and their interests, as well as those of the land, are concerned in removing all artificial obstructions. There is no longer any necessity for these, as steam-power can everywhere be substituted for water-mills, and the tedious delays of barges be superseded by the quicker and more certain conveyance by railways. The barge navigation was attended by one benefit, as, in order to maintain adequate depth of water, it was necessary to keep the bed of the river free from the natural growth of weeds which otherwise impede the current, and cause deposits of mud which gradually contract the outfall. Questions of compensation, however, arise when rights of any kind are touched, and hence the need of some authority to control and reconcile opposing interests.

The Inclosure Commissioners have power, upon application being made to them, to recommend the formation of drainage districts, which may embrace either the whole or a part of a river-basin. So far as their experience has gone, it is in favour of placing each river-basin as a whole system under competent authority, with power to that authority to form sub-districts for the management of each, with representatives at the general board which controls the whole. As the object is not to prevent floods, but to limit the period of their stagnation, it is seldom that any grand engineering operation is required. *Great engineering works seldom required.*

Another most useful branch of the office is the very extensive power entrusted to the Commissioners to carry out exchanges and partitions of lands. By their aid any two landowners can, *Power to exchange intermixed lands, inexpensive, and simple in its operation.*

at very trifling expense, correct any irregularity in the boundary of their respective estates, or even exchange entire farms or estates. This may be done without risk or investigation of title, by the simple process of attaching to the lands exchanged all the accidents of title, tenure, and incumbrance, which formerly belonged to each other. The only questions requiring the decision of the Commissioners are : Is the exchange beneficial to the two estates? Are the parcels proposed to be exchanged equal in value? or within one-eighth of an equality in value? When satisfied of this, the Commission authorises the exchange, and the one parcel immediately, for all purposes, takes the place of the other. So that if the title of either be thereafter found faulty, the person who may recover will have, not the land with the faulty title, but that which the Commissioners have put in its place, and clothed with all its liabilities. Certain notices must be given ; the order of exchange is not confirmed until three months after the notice, and if during that period any person dissents who is entitled to any estate in, or charge upon, either of the lands proposed to be exchanged, the Commissioners withhold their confirmation while the dissent continues. From time to time the powers of the Commission have been extended to comprise all cases omitted from the original statute. All hereditaments, corporeal and incorporeal, may now be exchanged with ease and at a very moderate cost. Inequality in value to the extent of an eighth may be compensated by a rent-charge annexed to the less valuable, and charged upon the more valuable property.

The extent to which this beneficial and inexpensive power is used is very considerable. It is mostly in the rectification of boundaries, or the exchange of intermixed lands, and in many cases to facilitate building operations, and embraces annually from 6,000 to 10,000 acres, having a value of from £400,000 to £500,000. *Extent to which it is made use of.*

CHAPTER IX.

WASTE LANDS AND COPYHOLDS.

Inclosure of waste lands: THE past result of the inclosure of waste lands under the control of the Government may be learned from a return to an Order of the House of Commons, made in 1873, which showed the extent of commons and common field lands then in England and Wales to be 2,632,000 acres, about one-fourteenth part of the whole surface of that country. Probably one million acres of the whole are capable of improvement by reclamation, drainage, or planting. Previous to the passing of the General Inclosure Act of 1845, 2,500 inclosures had been sanctioned by private Acts of Parliament, under which 2,142,000 acres of waste land were inclosed. *its extent,* The inclosures since 1845 have added 600,000 acres, so that up to the present time 2,757,000 acres altogether have been thus redeemed from waste. Besides this, a very large extent of country has been reclaimed without the intervention of Parliament.

The results of the inclosures since 1845 present some interesting facts in regard to the subdivision of land, and the addition made to the number of small landowners in the country, and the public works of improvement carried out under the process of inclosure, which are worthy of record. This is altogether independent of the individual and public advantages arising from the reclamation and agricultural improvement of the land itself. The 600,000 acres dealt with since 1845 have been divided among 26,000 separate owners, in an average proportion of 44½ acres to each lord of the manor, 24 acres to each common-right owner, and 10 acres to each purchaser of the lands sold to defray part of the expenses. In many cases the expenses were raised by rate among the persons interested, but this was optional, since such persons had the alternative of selling a portion of the land for that purpose. With that object 35,450 acres were sold, chiefly in small lots, to 3,500 purchasers. The lords of the

and results.

manors, 620 in number, received as compensation for their rights in the soil, on an average, about one-fifteenth of the acreage of the wastes. These wastes of manors were, under the Act of 1845, made subject to the setting out of allotments for public purposes, and in this respect were distinct from the commonable lands, which are undivided private property, and were not made subject to public allotments.

Quality and occupation of persons to whom waste lands passed. As this is the largest and most general distribution of land into small properties that has taken place in this country in recent times, it was desirable to know the quality and occupation of the persons into whose hands these lands have passed. To discover this, the legal description both of allottees and of purchasers of sale allotments, was taken from inclosures in which that description is given, one in each of the following counties, viz. Bucks, Cumberland, Chester, Devon, Essex, Hants, Herts, Lancaster, Norfolk, Oxford, Stafford, Sussex, Worcester, and, in Wales, Carnarvon and Carmarthen. Upon this basis, and so far as such an average can be accepted, the proportionate numbers of the different classes of the 26,000 landowners amongst whom the land has been divided are as follows :—Yeomen and farmers, 4,836; shopkeepers and tradesmen, 3,456; labourers and miners, 3,168; esquires, 2,624; widows, 2,016; gentlemen, 1,984; clergymen, 1,280; artisans, 1,067; spinsters, 800; charity trustees, 704; peers, baronets, and sons of peers, 576; professional men, 512; and about 3,000 others in gradually diminishing proportions, but comprising nearly every quality and calling, from the Crown to the mechanic, quarryman, and domestic servant. The influence of this change has not been confined to particular counties, but has been more or less felt in all. It has made an appreciable addition to the number of small landowners in England, bringing upon hitherto comparatively unproductive wastes the individual interest and intelligence of a numerous and varied body of persons, by whose industry the best of these lands have been made not only useful to their owners, but have become available for sale and purchase, and, in their improved condition, for bearing their just share of county and parish rates and public taxes.

<small>Extent of public roads constructed,</small>

More than two thousand miles of public roads have been constructed in connection with these enclosures since 1845, at the cost of the common-right owners, in addition to the numerous accommodation roads set out for their special use in giving convenient access to their several allotments. Other works of a public nature, such as embanking and straightening the course of rivers connected with inclosures, have

<small>and value of lands devoted to public objects, at the cost of the owners of common rights, equal to one-eighth of whole value of the land inclosed.</small>

been executed. The value of lands devoted to public objects, at the cost of the owners of common rights, is equal to one-eighth of the whole value of the land inclosed.

The total estimated value of the wastes inclosed amounts to £6,140,000. The value of the land taken from the best of this for public purposes (comprising land for recreation, field-gardens, public quarries, fuel, schools and churches, burial-grounds, public roads, and other purposes) has been estimated at £282,140. To this must be added the cash, raised by rate, or sale of property, and expended on the construction of public roads and other public works connected with inclosures, £473,500, making together, £755,640. Comparing this with the fee-simple value above mentioned, it appears that nearly one-eighth of the whole value of the wastes inclosed has, under the direction of the Commissioners, and with the assent of the proprietary interests, been devoted to objects of public utility and convenience. Thus, in the course of one generation, an extent of land equal to that of a county has been redeemed from a condition of waste, and has been divided among a far larger and more varied body of landowners than that of any county in England. Valuable public roads of great extent have been constructed, opening up for business and pleasure many otherwise inaccessible localities, and at no cost to the public. The area of production and employment has been increased, and in the same proportion that of public and local taxation has been extended. A great number of small landed properties have been created, and labourers' field-gardens in the rural districts have been afforded in larger proportion to the extent of the land than appears by the Agricultural Returns to exist elsewhere in England.

Though the best of the land was probably first dealt with, there can be little doubt that much of that which still remains uninclosed may be advantageously brought under the operation of the new law of 1876, which, in the altered state of the circumstances since 1845, provides more fully for the public interests of the neighbourhood, and especially of large populations; and at the same time may yet be found, in less populous quarters, the useful instrument of adding some considerable extent of available land to the solid resources of the country.

Enfranchisement of copyhold lands or buildings. Lands or houses held by copyhold tenure may be enfranchised through the copyhold department of this Commission. These are held by record in the book of the lord of a manor, anciently on certain terms of service, now commuted into a money payment. The tenants of a manor, which was held by the lord from the Crown under ancient grant, gradually acquired the right to be placed on the court roll of the lord on the same conditions as their predecessors, and became entitled to demand copies of these conditions, which, so long as they were fulfilled, gave them a title to their estates. The conditions of the tenure are governed by the customs of the manor as shown in the rolls of the Manor Courts, and by constant and immemorial usage; and the title is simply a copy of the court roll, authenticated by the steward of the manor. Two conditions are essential: first, that the lands are parcel of, and situated within, the manor; and secondly, that they have been demised, or are demisable by copy of court roll immemorially.

The ease with which a title can be given is the only advantage which this kind of tenure possesses, the uncertain nature of its services, reliefs, escheats, fines and heriots, and rights to timber, being a great obstacle to any kind of improvement. In 1841, the Legislature, with a view of removing these disadvantages, passed an Act for commuting manorial rights, and facilitating the enfranchisement of copyhold property. This was amended and extended by subsequent

Acts of the Legislature. Since 1841 upwards of twelve thousand enfranchisements have been completed under the Copyhold Acts, and they are now proceeding, through the instrumentality of the Copyhold Commission, at an average rate of 600 a year. Besides these, a very large number have been effected throughout the different parts of the country, without the intervention of the office, owing to the stimulus to voluntary enfranchisement given by the Copyhold Acts. But though the number seems large, it represents probably but a moderate proportion of the whole, as wherever there is a manor there are many copyhold properties; and much yet remains to be accomplished before this injurious and obstructive kind of tenure shall altogether cease to exist. The Copyhold Commission was formed with the intention gradually to abolish copyhold tenure, beginning by offering facilities for voluntary enfranchisement, after which it should proceed to its object of extinction on the compulsory principle. Accordingly, after ten years' trial of facilities under the voluntary system, compulsory powers were given to either

Number completed.

lord or tenant to demand enfranchisement, with further facilities again in 1858, which led to a rapid increase in the number of enfranchisements. Under the present Acts either lord or tenant (except where the copyhold is held without a right of renewal) may now apply to the Copyhold Commissioners to compel enfranchisement upon terms to be fixed by two valuers, one appointed by each, or by their umpire. And in small cases, not exceeding £20 of annual value, the amount may be assessed by a single valuer, nominated by the Justices of the locality.

The complete extinction of copyhold tenure is still far from accomplishment. And a great bar will be presented to the profitable use of copyhold property so long as any considerable extent of the land of this country, embracing a vast number of the smaller estates and houses, remains subject to manorial fines, whether certain or arbitrary; to joint rights in timber, under which the tenant cannot cut without leave of the lord, nor the lord enter the land to cut without leave of the tenant; and to vexatious

Complete extinction desirable.

demands for heriots, and a species of control worse than double ownership. These are evils naturally most felt in the populous parts of the country. The Copyhold Commission has now been in operation for thirty-five years, so that full time has been given to prepare and provide for the final extinction of this kind of tenure, as originally contemplated by Parliament. The simplest mode of doing so would be by enacting that within some definite number of years, say thirty, all copyholds then existing should become freehold. Till the termination of that period the right of either party to compel enfranchisement should continue, and the obvious interest of the lords to make the most of their opportunity would quickly bring about this transformation.

<small>Mode of accomplishing this.</small>

The Tithe department of this Commission also administers questions connected with tithes for the support of religion.

CHAPTER X.

CHURCH, CROWN, AND CHARITY ESTATES.

IN the early period of Christianity in this country, among other ecclesiastical laws introduced from the neighbouring Continent, the Scriptural principle of reserving for the support of religion a tenth part of the produce of industry was enjoined. This included not only a tenth part of the produce of the crops and stock payable in gross, but also a tenth of the clear gains from manual occupations and trades. This large proportion of the total produce of those countries which had embraced Christianity was apportioned, more than a thousand years ago, into four divisions: one to maintain the edifice of the church, the second to support the poor, the third the bishops, and the fourth the parochial clergy. Originally all the land in the country was titheable except such as belonged to the Crown and to the Church itself. At the time of the Reformation, much of the Church lands in this country passed into the

Tithes for support of religion in England:

hands of laymen, and continued exempt from tithe, and from various other causes a considerable proportion of the lands of the country has become exempted. As the country became more populous, and its demands upon the produce of the soil more difficult to meet, the payment of tithes in kind was found a great hindrance to improved agriculture, as men were naturally unwilling to expend capital for the purpose of increasing the produce, while others who ran no risk, and bore no part of the toil, had a right to share in that increase. Forty years ago it was determined that this should cease, and it was enacted that, instead of payment in kind, tithes should be commuted into a payment in money, calculated on the average receipts of the preceding seven years, the annual money value to vary according to the annual price of corn on a septennial average, but the quantity of corn then ascertained to remain for ever as the tithe of the parish.

<small>commuted from payment in kind to a money payment.</small>

A very important change of principle here took place. Up to that time, the income of the Church increased with the increased value yielded by the land, the original object that the Church should progress in material resources in equal proportion with the land being thus maintained. From 1836 that increment was stopped. Since that time the land rental of England has risen 50 per cent., and all that portion of the increase which previous to 1836 would have gone to the Church has gone to the landowners. A tenth of that would not, however, by any means adequately represent the loss to the Church and the gain to the landowners; for the tithe in kind was the tenth of the gross produce, which was equal to much more than a tenth of the rent of arable land. In 1836 the money value of the tithe, as compared with the land rental, was as four millions sterling to thirty-three. In 1876 the tithe was still four millions, but the land rental had risen to fifty. If the old principle of participation had continued, the annual income of the Church would now have been two millions greater than it is. Neither party anticipated a result to such an extent when the Tithe Commutation Act was passed, for not for twenty years after that

Unexpected effect of this, in preventing a rise in the income of the Church, and increasing that of the landowners.

time had the rent of land in England recovered the heavy fall it experienced at the close of the war in 1815. It was not until the vast development of industry, under a policy of Free Trade, had so increased the general prosperity, that the value and rent of land began steadily to rise. It then became plain that under the operation of a law intended simply to encourage agricultural improvement, the community, represented by the Church, are gradually losing a part of their natural inheritance. The same change is in operation in the vicinity of the great cities and towns, where population and wealth increase and accumulate. An acre of land in such situations, which yielded in its natural state a rent to the landowner of £3, and to the tithe-owner of 10s., when converted to building may produce a ground rent of £300, besides the reversion to the landowner at the end of a long lease of the whole of the property erected on it by his lessee. No doubt, since the Reformation, the Church has been limited by law to the agricultural increased produce, and was not entitled to demand a share of the building value. But it was not contemplated that the landowners should thus obtain the whole growing value of the land without leaving any part of it for the support of religion. The operation of this change has been chiefly in favour of the better class of lands, those which from their quality and position have risen most in value. On the poorest kinds of arable land—the cold clays, and the thinnest chalk—the increased cost of labour has, in some exceptional cases, brought about a lowering of rent, while the tithe can undergo no diminution. The landowner in such case has to bear the loss, just as in the other he gets the gain.

In a country like this, in which the inevitable tendency of increasing wealth leads to the gradual diminution of small estates, there would be some considerable loss to the ranks of small resident proprietors by any change which should lead to the absorption of Church property. In every parish of the kingdom there is a resident landowner, who, as the clergyman of the parish, receives in residence, glebe, and tithe, about a tenth part of its rental, which he spends within

Parish clergy equivalent in number to more than one-fourth of the resident landowners, over £200 a year.

it, and in return for which he is the minister of rich and poor. The number may be about 12,000 in England alone, with an average annual value of £300. As their income is in no way affected by the question of rent, their position is one of perfect impartiality between landowners and their tenants, and they are the natural referees of the poorer inhabitants. In proportion to the whole number of landowners in England the removal of this numerous body would strike out more than a fourth of those receiving above £200 a year, and probably much more than one-fourth of the resident landowners. This, irrespective of the question of religion, would be a change of great magnitude in its social effect, which deserves careful consideration.

CROWN ESTATES.

Her Majesty's Woods, Forests, and Land revenue,

Besides the domain and Great Park attached to the Royal Castle of Windsor, 14,000 acres in extent, there are comprised in the Royal patrimony upwards of 70,000 acres of land in the kingdom let in farms to agricultural tenants, and also house property in London, and land let on building leases, and considerably more than 100,000 acres of Royal forests. For the last twenty years this great property has been managed by two Commissioners, under the superintendence of Her Majesty's Treasury, with great judgment and care, and at the moderate cost of less than 3 per cent. on the total receipts. The gross revenue has for some years shown a steady annual increase, and now amounts to £469,000. A large expenditure is annually made in maintaining and improving the property, but the surplus now paid annually to the Exchequer has risen above, and is likely to continue more and more to exceed the annual amount of the Civil List. This is a sum assured by Parliament to the Sovereign, at the beginning of each reign, to defray the expenses of the Royal Household, by an arrangement continued from Sovereign to Sovereign from the time of the Revolution in 1688. The surplus income from the hereditary estates of the Crown, which was then precarious and uncertain, is by this arrangement during the reign of the Sovereign

now yield a net revenue to the public Exchequer exceeding the amount of the Civil List.

paid into the public Exchequer, and a fixed sum of £385,000 is, in lieu of it, annually paid to the Queen for the maintenance of her State, and for the salaries and expenses of Her Majesty's Household. In the period of forty years since the commencement of the present reign, all expenses, both public and private, have largely increased, but no new demand on that account has been made on the public for an increase of the Civil List. And as the hereditary estates are now yielding to the public Exchequer more than the Exchequer pays to the Queen, the remarkable and probably unique example is presented in this country of a great Sovereign whose household and Royal dignity are thus maintained without taxing her subjects.

I am indebted to the Earl of Powis for the following interesting particulars in the business relations of the Crown with its agricultural tenants :—The average rental of the agricultural land of the Crown Estates is at present rather more than 32s. 6d. per acre. Nearly the whole of it is let in farms of various sizes, on agricultural leases of 21 years' duration, subject to the

General conditions on which the Crown Farms are let.

reservation of all trees and substrata. The tenants are to reside on the premises; to cultivate according to the best mode of husbandry in the district; within the last three years of the termination of the lease not to sow two white crops in succession, or to plant on the same land more than one crop of potatoes. The tenants to be entitled to one-half of the money expended by them in the last year of the term in the purchase of linseed, cotton-cake, and rape-cake consumed on the premises, but not to an amount exceeding one-half of the average expenditure for such articles during each of the three preceding years. The right of shooting and sporting is not reserved from the tenants, except under very special circumstances. New buildings are constructed, and existing buildings improved, and under-drainage, roads, and other permanent improvements executed at the cost of the Crown. Terms of renewal are proposed to desirable tenants, two years before the expiration of lease.

Many private landowners would find just and suggestive hints in these arrangements.

CHARITY ESTATES.

Charity Estates: The value and extent of land held in trust for charities, in England alone, is very considerable. Inclusive of rent-charges and fixed annual payments, the gross annual rental exceeds £1,558,000, derived from 524,000 acres of land, and the houses built thereon. Besides this, the Charity Trusts possess in Government Stock and other personalty, nearly £20,000,000, yield-

their value. ing an annual income of £640,000. Their total income from real and personal property is thus close upon £2,200,000.

This great property is held in separate endowments in all parts of England, in number estimated at about 50,000, which are administered by various bodies of trustees, such as Municipal Trustees, Ministers, and Parish Officers, and in many cases by persons who may be termed private trustees, or such as are not trustees in virtue of holding any especial office. These have been placed by Parliament under the general superintendence of a Government Department, the Charity Commission, which reports annually to Parliament upon the administration of the charities over which they possess necessary power of control.

The principal objects to which the funds were appropriated by the founders of the charities are education, apprenticing, and advancement of orphans; endowment of clergy, lecturers, and for sermons; Church purposes and repairs; maintenance of Dissenting places of worship and their ministers; public parochial uses; support of almshouses and pensioners; distribution of articles in kind and money; medical hospitals and dispensaries. The property which has thus in the past been voluntarily devoted by benevolent persons as an endowment for charitable objects in England, is equal to more than one-half of that possessed by the Established Church. If we add the amount annually expended in the United Kingdom on the relief of the poor and in aid of education, it appears that the annual expenditure on objects of charity exceeds the whole cost of the civil administration of the country.

Their magnitude compared with the cost of the civil administration.

CHAPTER XI.

THE FUTURE.

Home production of bread and meat limited.

THE question of the future for the landed interests and the public, in regard to the supply of food, remains to be considered. The landlord and the tenant will settle the rent between them: with returning activity in trade the wages of labour will increase, and that will be followed by increased consumption of bread and meat. Hitherto, there has been no corresponding rise in the price of bread with that of meat, because wheat has been poured in upon us from fertile lands in distant countries, where the cost of cultivation is small. The effect of this on home agriculture has been to limit any increase on our production of corn. In ten years, indeed, the growth of corn has declined five per cent., the diminution being entirely in wheat, and that chiefly in Ireland. In other respects the annual home growth of corn keeps steady, barley alone showing a gradual increase. The production of bread and meat within these islands appears to have nearly reached its limit. The dairy and market-garden system, fresh milk and butter, and vegetables, and hay and straw, are every year enlarging their circle around the seat of increasing populations. These are the articles which can least bear distant transport, and, therefore, are likely longest to withstand the influence of foreign competition.

This country is becoming every ten years less and less of a farm, and more and more of a meadow, a garden, and a playground. The deer forest, and grouse, in the higher and wilder parts of the country, and the picturesque commons in the more populous districts, are already, in many cases, not only more attractive, but more remunerative in health and enjoyment, than they probably would be if subjected to costly improvement by drainage, or by being broken up for cultivation. The poor clay soils, which are expensive to cultivate, and meagre

Country becoming less of a farm and more of a garden.

in yield, will be gradually all laid to grass, and the poorer soils of every kind, upon which the costs of cultivation bear a high proportion to the produce, will probably follow the same rule. During the last ten years the permanent pasture in Great Britain has, chiefly from this cause, been increased by more than one million acres.

Population at present rate of increase.

On the other hand the population is multiplying at the rate of 350,000 a year, nearly a thousand a day. Their consumption of food improves, not only in proportion to their increase in numbers, but also with the augmenting scale of wages. Twenty-five years ago the agricultural population rarely could afford to eat butchers' meat more than once a week. Some of them now have it every day, and as the condition of the rest of the people has improved in an equal degree, the increased consumption of food in this country has been prodigious. In addition to the whole of our home produce, we imported in 1877 foreign food and corn of the value of one hundred millions sterling, two-thirds of which was in corn, and one-third live and dead meat. It has become a vast trade, embracing not only the nearer ports of Europe, but those of India, Australia, and America, which in corn has increased threefold, and in meat and provisions sixfold. If this goes on at the same progressive rate for the next twenty years, we shall have forty millions of people to feed, which will tax still more the resources of all those countries which have hitherto sent us their surplus, and can hardly fail to be attended by a considerable increase of the price of provisions.

Will in twenty years be forty millions, causing a further rise in prices.

It would seem, under such circumstances, not difficult to forecast the future condition of the landed interests in this country. The position of the landowners is a truly advantageous one if they rightly appreciate, and faithfully execute, the public responsibilities of their position. Their property is the only exchangeable article within the British Isles that admits of no increase in extent. So long as England continues the centre of the Empire, the surplus wealth of her great dependencies will flow hither, and aid in that accumulation of

Prospects of Landowner good,

K

wealth which is at once the source and reward of industry. A large portion of that wealth will constantly be seeking investment in land. The climate of this country is not only one of the healthiest in the world, but it admits of out-of-door occupations and amusements for a greater number of days in the year, and thus promotes the attractions of a country life to a greater extent than is found elsewhere. For many centuries landed property has been more secure here than in other countries, and a sense of, and respect for, individual liberty, and obedience to law, better understood. All circumstances combine to increase the future value of land in this country.

of Tenant-farmer more doubtful. The prospects of the tenant-farmer, the second of our landed interests, are by no means so encouraging. While competition for the purchase of land is advantageous to the landowner, competition for its occupation diminishes the margin of the tenant's profit. And he has to contend against it on both sides, for other attractions and the facilities of locomotion have so altered the position of the labourer, that he presses for higher wages. When the landowner is offered a higher rent, and the labourer higher wages, or a better chance of improving his condition in our colonies, the position of the middleman who has to meet the demands of both seems a difficult one. He, like any other capitalist, may no doubt withdraw it from an unprofitable business, and carry it to some other country where good land is plentiful and cheap, and where he may become a landowner, and escape at least one of the competing forces to which he is here exposed.

But if the business has these disadvantages, how happens it that there is such competition for the occupation of land? It has many attractions. A country life, personal ease and independence, part ownership of agricultural property, a comfortable home where most of the necessaries of life are obtained at producers' prices, and a freedom from that need to study the feelings and prejudices of customers to which most professions and trades are exposed. The farmer is master of his position, has a certain weight in his parish and neighbourhood, and is looked up to by the people in his employment. Men in all ranks of life in these islands are attracted by the occupation of a country life. When they become rich enough they buy land, or if they cannot afford to buy they hire it. There is thus a constant pressure of competition to which the tenant-farmer is exposed, and from which, as years go by, it is impossible he can escape, except by becoming an owner of land, or by securing himself in a lengthened leasehold tenure. No tenancy-at-will, or with a year's notice, however favourable the conditions of compensation for unexhausted improvements, can give the farmer security beyond the year. The Agricultural Holdings Bill, with two instead of one year's notice, would be a vast improvement on the common practice of yearly tenancy, and so far as it goes will bear good fruit in forcing landowners and their tenants to adopt written agreements on a sounder basis. But the sooner the principle of security of possession, for a definite and lengthened term, becomes generally recognised in England, the better will

His duty to protect himself by a definite and lengthened term.

it be for the individual and public interests. Writing with the responsibility of a practical experience of forty years, and with a general knowledge both personally and officially of the agriculture of the United Kingdom, and of the relations between landlord and tenant, I venture, with all becoming respect for the opinions of others, to say with confidence that the good understanding which has hitherto as a rule protected the English farmer under a yearly tenancy, will not for many years longer be able to withstand the inevitable spread and pressure of competition. However unpalatable the truth, the relation is and must become one of business, and not merely of mutual confidence.

Increasing pressure of competition.

There are two modes, as I have said, of meeting the difficulty, and we may shortly consider the first, that of the tenant becoming himself the owner of his farm. The Irish Land Act provides for such a change, and it has been recommended by an influential committee of the House of Commons that enlarged facilities for this object should be afforded in that country by an increased proportion of the price being

Facilities given by Government for purchase in Ireland.

If extended to England and Scotland would be more rapidly appropriated.

advanced out of the public Treasury. If the security for repayment of the advance is good in Ireland, it would be doubly good in England and Scotland, and if the infusion amongst the body of landowners in the sister country of some proportion of the Irish tenantry is regarded as beneficial, much more would such advantageous results be likely to be secured by the addition of a body of more educated and enterprising agriculturists to the landlords of Great Britain. There is not a single reason in favour of exceptional aid from the public Treasury for Ireland that is not equally applicable to the rest of the United Kingdom, and, if such aid can be given without injury to other interests, the extension of the "Bright Clauses" of the Irish Land Act to England and Scotland would be followed by a much more rapid appropriation of their advantages to the farmer than they have yet met with in Ireland. There are landed estates in almost every county in Great Britain, coming from time to time into the market, which are not sufficiently residential to attract great capitalists, but which would be very eligible investments for resident tenant-farmers, if they were placed on a par with their Irish brethren in the facilities offered by the Legislature for finding capital to buy them. Outside of such exceptional assistance a British farmer can still employ his limited capital to greater advantage by hiring farms than by buying them.

The second mode will probably, therefore, be found in the end the most generally applicable, viz., that of a lengthened leasehold tenure. Time is required in the operations of agriculture. Drainage, clean cultivation, manures of the more lasting kind, and the costly and skilful formation of a suitable live-stock, each demand a considerable period of years for profitable realisation. A well-organised farm is not only the source of employment to the labour and trades of the neighbourhood, but a school of practical education in which these are trained in the details of work, and become apt in the execution of the views of their employer. Both employer and employed form family connections and local associations, and have their due place

Time essential in the operations of agriculture.

in the economy of the parish and district. These should not be liable to be lightly broken by the act of an inconsiderate landowner, or his agent. In some English counties, and notably on the Crown estates in various parts of the country, and on Lord Leicester's fine farms in Norfolk, leases of twenty and twenty-one years have long been given.

The system may be said to be universal in Scotland, where the principle has been recognised for several generations. In Ireland, as has been previously shown, leases for lives, leases for ever even, are not uncommon, but the rule, now becoming general, is that of leases for twenty-one or thirty-one years. In farms under £100 rental, where no lease for the usual statutory term of years is given, there is a security against "disturbance" or removal, by very stringent conditions upon the landowner, under the late Irish Land Act. No such legal obligations are imposed in England or Scotland, where, on this very important point, the farmer is left, like other members of the community, to make his own bargain.

Security against disturbance in Ireland.

The example of a lease which is equitable to both sides, and under which the farmer obtains reasonable security to continue good cultivation from the commencement to the close, is to be found in the farm lease of the Earl of Leicester. It fully recognises that continuance of interests to which I have referred, but most properly leaves both parties free to withdraw from the contract at its termination. The tenancy is for twenty years from the 11th day of October. It is to be terminable at the end of sixteen years, at the request of the tenant and with the consent of the landlord, the intention being that, if both parties desire it, a new lease may be granted from the end of the sixteenth year for a fresh term of twenty years, at the old rent for the first four (which completes the original term), and for the remainder at such a rent as may be agreed on. The tenant is to cultivate and manage the farm during the first sixteen years according to his own judgment, and to dispose of the produce as he finds best. A power is reserved to interpose if this freedom

Lord Leicester's lease an admirable example in its chief features, which admit of freedom of management, and provide for renewal without exposure to undue competition.

should be misused. During the last four years, if a renewed lease is not entered upon, he is to bring the farm into the ordinary four-course or Norfolk system, with proper conditions of payment for unexhausted manures. He is to effectually destroy all rabbits on his farm, and other usual conditions, adapted to local circumstances, complete the arrangement. The leading principle of this admirable lease is applicable to all parts of the United Kingdom. It supplies the great defect of most leases, and especially those of Scotland, in giving entire freedom to the action of the farmer in the cultivation and disposal of the produce up to four years preceding the termination, when an opportunity is given to both to consider the question of renewal. If that is satisfactorily arranged, the same freedom of management continues, and the farmer is not exposed to that harassing competition, the fear of which compels him to reduce the condition of his land in the closing years of his tenancy. If, on the other hand, it is found expedient that a change should be made, the farm is brought into the usual course of husbandry.

In regard to the future of the third branch of the landed interests, the agricultural labourer, his prospects will now harmonise with the general prosperity of the country, and the standard of wages. There is no impediment in his way to move to a better field of employment, either in this country or abroad. Great encouragement is offered, and cheap transit, to agricultural labourers, by several of the colonies. The extensive use of machinery in the processes of farming has greatly lightened the severity of labour, and stimulated the intelligence of the workman. Co-operative farming has been much recommended, but in one instance only, that I have heard of, successfully carried into practice. The labourer is now much more independent of local employment, and his position in a wealthy country like this will enable him in its future progress to obtain his due share of the rewards of industry and

The Labourer.

His work lightened and intelligence stimulated by extended use of machinery.

skill. The extension to the counties of household suffrage will, ere long, give him that political position to which he is equally entitled with his brethren, the artisans and labourers, who are householders in towns.

APPENDIX.

THE following tables have been carefully compiled from authentic sources and Parliamentary Returns, and may be found useful for reference :—

Table showing the Rent of Cultivated Land, the Price of Provisions, the Wages of the Agricultural Labourer, the Rent of Cottages, and the average Produce of Wheat, in three periods during the last hundred years in England.

	1770.		1850.		1878.	
	s.	d.	s.	d.	s.	d.
Rent of Cultivated Land per acre	13	0	27	0	30	0
Price of Bread per lb.	0	1½	0	1¼	0	1½
,, Meat ,,	0	3¼	0	5	0	9
,, Butter ,,	0	6	1	0	1	8
Agricultural Labourer's Wages per week	7	3	9	7	14	0
Rent of Labourer's Cottage ,,	0	8	1	5	2	0
Produce of Wheat, per acre, in bushels	Bushels. 23		Bushels. 26½		Bushels. 28	

Acreage under Crops, and Number of Live-stock in the United Kingdom.

	Corn.	Green Crops.	Permanent Pasture (exclusive of Moor and Mountain).	Horses.	Cattle.	Sheep.	Pigs (exclusive of those kept in Towns and by Cottagers).
1867	11,432,503	4,951,896	22,052,510	...	8,731,473	33,817,951	4,221,100
1868	11,659,855	4,865,057	22,164,584	...	9,083,416	35,607,812	3,189,167
1869	12,000,111	5,095,933	22,811,284	...	9,078,282	34,250,272	3,028,394
1870	11,755,053	5,107,135	22,085,295	2,631,206	9,235,052	32,786,783	3,650,730
1871	11,833,243	5,271,398	22,525,761	2,698,223	9,346,216	31,403,500	4,136,616
1872	11,698,245	5,111,994	22,838,178	2,715,307	9,718,505	32,246,642	4,178,000
1873	11,422,532	4,971,112	23,363,990	2,732,831	10,153,670	33,982,404	3,513,532
1874	11,364,834	4,957,683	23,680,416	2,762,148	10,281,036	34,837,597	3,537,354
1875	11,399,030	5,057,029	23,772,602	2,790,851	10,162,787	33,491,948	3,495,167
1876	11,064,946	4,960,166	24,053,273	2,834,000	9,997,189	32,252,579	3,734,429
1877	11,103,196	4,961,691	23,903,314	2,866,000	9,731,537	32,220,067	3,984,447
1878	...	...	...	...	9,723,227	32,491,504	3,752,777

APPENDIX.

Quantities of Foreign Wheat, and other kinds of Grain, and Value of Grain, and Live-stock, and Provisions, imported into the United Kingdom, and Value per head of Population, in each of the years 1858 to 1877.

	Wheat.	Other kinds.	Total.	Value of Corn, Grain, and Flour.	Value of Live Cattle, Sheep, and Pigs.	Value of Dead Meat and Provisions.	Total Value of Corn, Cattle, and Provisions.	Value per head of Population.
	Cwts.	Cwts.	Cwts.	£	£	£	£	£ s. d.
1858	18,380,782	25,358,418	43,739,210	20,164,811	1,390,068	4,343,592	25,898,471	0 18 3
1859	17,337,329	22,327,016	39,664,345	18,044,203	1,634,766	4,680,629	24,359,598	0 17 0
1860	25,484,151	30,721,487	56,205,638	31,676,353	2,117,860	8,076,304	41,871,517	1 9 1
1861	29,955,532	34,048,077	64,003,609	34,922,095	2,211,969	9,151,078	46,285,142	1 11 11
1862	41,033,503	33,071,858	74,105,361	37,774,148	1,888,236	10,630,734	50,293,118	1 14 5
1863	24,364,171	35,467,874	59,832,045	25,956,520	2,655,072	10,841,324	39,452,916	1 6 10
1864	23,196,714	23,822,008	47,018,722	19,882,181	4,275,322	12,157,010	36,314,513	1 4 6
1865	20,962,963	28,529,148	49,492,111	20,725,483	6,548,413	12,667,838	39,941,734	1 6 9
1866	23,156,329	39,794,780	62,951,109	30,049,655	5,839,058	13,483,715	49,372,428	1 12 10
1867	34,645,569	31,378,924	66,024,593	41,368,349	4,148,382	12,489,331	58,006,062	1 18 3
1868	32,639,768	34,367,601	67,007,369	39,432,624	2,698,496	13,277,683	55,408,803	1 16 2
1869	37,695,828	42,226,108	79,921,936	37,351,089	5,299,087	15,189,933	57,840,109	1 17 5
1870	30,901,229	43,202,284	74,103,513	34,170,221	4,654,905	14,773,712	53,598,838	1 14 4
1871	39,389,803	44,568,186	83,957,989	42,691,464	5,663,150	16,593,668	64,948,282	2 1 3
1872	42,127,726	60,068,508	102,196,234	51,228,816	4,394,850	18,604,273	72,227,934	2 6 6
1873	43,863,098	50,538,249	94,401,347	51,737,811	5,418,584	23,854,967	81,011,362	2 10 5
1874	41,527,638	51,470,198	92,997,836	51,070,202	5,265,041	25,224,958	81,560,201	2 10 4
1875	51,876,517	55,645,125	107,521,642	53,086,691	7,326,288	25,880,806	86,293,785	2 12 8
1876	44,454,657	73,520,939	117,975,596	51,812,438	7,260,119	29,851,647	88,924,204	2 13 9
1877	54,269,800	70,358,393	124,628,193	63,536,322	6,012,564	30,144,013	99,692,899	2 19 7

APPENDIX.

Table showing the Annual Yield of Wheat per acre in the United Kingdom during each of the last thirty years, and in three periods of ten years each, reckoning 28 bushels as an average crop, and representing that by the number 100.

Years.	Produce per Acre.	
	Each Year.	In Ten Years.
1849	123	
1850	102	
1851	110	
1852	79	
1853	71	
1854	127	
1855	96	
1856	96	
1857	124	
1858	116	1,044
1859	92	
1860	78	
1861	92	
1862	108	
1863	141	
1864	127	
1865	110	
1866	90	
1867	74	
1868	126	1,038
1869	102	
1870	112	
1871	90	
1872	92	
1873	80	
1874	106	
1875	78	
1876	76	
1877	74	
1878	108	918
In 30 years		3,000